D0702363

Against All Odds

Speaking Naturally with Idioms

Marie Hutchison Eichler
University of California, Irvine

HEINLE & HEINLE PUBLISHERS
A Division of Wadsworth, Inc.
Boston, Massachusetts 02116

To Arthur, and other obstinate creatures.

Director: Laurie E. Likoff
Full-Service Manager: Michael Weinstein
Production Coordinator: Cynthia Funkhouser
Text Design: Eliz. Anne O'Donnell
Cover Design: Caliber Design Planning
Text Illustrations: Annette Jane Slezak and Julie Gillman
Photos: Chapters 2, 3, 4, 9, 11, and 13: Beryl Goldberg, Chapter 5: © *Hank deLespinasse.* 1988. All rights reserved.
Production: Ruttle, Shaw & Wetherill, Inc.
Printer and Binder: Malloy Lithographing

Against All Odds: Speaking Naturally with Idioms

ISBN 0-8384-2855-X

Library of Congress Cataloging-in-Publication Data

Eichler, Marie Hutchison.
    Against all odds : speaking naturally with idioms / Marie H.
Eichler.
        p.   cm.

    1. English language—Textbooks for foreign speakers.   2. English
language—Spoken English.   3. English language—Idioms.   I. Title.
PE1128.E3498   1990
428.3'4—dc20   90-22373
                                                                 CIP

94 93   9 8 7 6 5 4 3

Contents

CHAPTER 1: Time   1

on time • ahead of time • from now on • in time • off and on • just around the corner • every so often • day in and day out • every now and then • so far • once in a while • in the long run • for good • for the time being • right away

CHAPTER 2: Plans and Schedules   15

be about to • keep track of • look forward to • call off • fall through • fall behind • catch up on • put off • on the spur of the moment • behind schedule • around the clock • make good time • carry out • bring up to date • move back • move up

CHAPTER 3: Cooperation   27

right-hand man/woman • hand in hand • give a hand • meet one halfway • come through for • give a break • bend over backwards to • do a favor • take turns • pull together • give and take • help out • see eye to eye • back up • keep one's word

CHAPTER 4: Finances   41

lay off • in the red/black • make ends meet • be/go broke • do without • live it up • run out of • get out from under • make a living • run • land on one's feet • break even • be a steal • wear out • come up in the world

CHAPTER 13: Creativity   175

fix up   •   put our/your heads together   •   come up with   •   make do with   •
make up   •   hit on   •   make a breakthrough   •   kick around   •   work out   •
think up   •   draw up   •   take shape   •   dry run   •   dream up   •   lose one's
touch

CHAPTER 14: Control   189

keep an eye on   •   keep tabs on   •   take charge of   •   take in hand   •   get out
of hand   •   keep in line   •   take over   •   keep a lid on   •   put one's foot
down   •   stand for   •   check up on   •   be at the mercy of   •   go off the deep
end   •   lose track of   •   get carried away

CHAPTER 15: Foolishness   205

blow   •   cut corners   •   let down   •   mess up   •   goof off   •   fool around   •
lose one's head   •   get in trouble   •   get on one's nerves   •   have a screw
loose   •   make fun of   •   knock it off   •   make waves   •   make a fool of   •
get caught red-handed   •   get away with

Glossary   218
Answer Key   226

Introduction to the Text

Against All Odds is an idioms text designed to help high-intermediate and advanced ESL/EFL students (TOEFL 450–550) to develop more natural-sounding spoken English and to improve their ability to understand naturally spoken English. Every effort has been made to include idioms that ESL/EFL students will find useful in their everyday lives and will often encounter in conversation with native English speakers. The number of idioms per chapter has purposely been limited to 15–17 so that students can truly acquire them for active use. In addition, each chapter's idioms are grouped semantically to further facilitate acquisition of the idioms. While some of the idioms are the traditional phrasal verbs, most are not.

Each chapter is composed of the following 11 sections:

An introductory proverb: Each chapter begins with a popular proverb or saying, an explanation of its meaning, and brief discussion questions. This is designed to be used as a warm-up for the semantic category of the chapter.

Get Ready: In this pre-listening section, students prepare to hear a long conversation by first looking at a photograph or illustration that represents the action of the conversation and inducing information about the speakers' situation from the questions given.

Get the Gist: After hearing the conversation one time, students answer comprehension questions that are designed to ensure that they have understood the main points of the conversation. Students can then concentrate on the idioms when they listen again.

Zero In: During this exercise, students hear the conversation again, perhaps twice more in early chapters, listening especially for the underlined idioms, to determine the most likely meaning for that idiom from the list given. This exercise allows students to induce the meanings of the idioms, develop their listening skills, and develop an ability to determine the meanings of idioms from context— an important skill in a language that has thousands of idioms.

Get Your Bearings: In this part of each chapter, students start to become more familiar with the idioms' meanings and structural requirements as they work at written exercises.

Tune In: Here, students refine their ability to hear and understand spoken English that contains idioms. While all "Tune In" listening sections include idioms from the present chapter, some spiral in idioms from previous chapters as well. These are marked with an Ⓡ.

Get Down to Business: As the title implies, this part of each chapter is the beginning of the "heart" of the text, where students act out roleplays using idioms from the present chapter. The opportunity for interaction that these roleplays provide allows students to develop their English fluency and naturalness and to better retain the idioms.

Put It All Together: Roleplays continue in this section, this time incorporating idioms from many of the previous chapters as well. This spiraling of idioms facilitates retention of idioms in the entire text.

Keep the Ball Rolling: Each chapter culminates in a problem-solving or discussion activity, again based on idioms from the present and previous chapters.

Put a Fine Point on Them: Definitions, grammatical notes, and sentence-level contexts for the idioms can be found here.

Check It Out: Here the conversation from the *Get the Gist/Zero In* sections is available for students' scrutiny.

Using the Text

The text is organized so that it can meet a variety of curricular demands. However, it should be noted that idioms from previous chapters are often spiraled into new chapters' long conversations, listening passages, and written exercises.

The Proverb: This part can be done as a quick class warm-up or in small groups or pairs, as time allows.

Get Ready/Get the Gist/Zero In/Tune In: These pre-listening and listening exercises can be done in class with the aid of the TAPE SCRIPT or a tape recorder, or in the language laboratory class with the accompanying tape. Students can also be assigned to do "Get the Gist," "Zero In," and "Tune In" in the language laboratory for homework after "Get Ready" has been done in class.

Get Your Bearings: Where time is limited, these exercises can be assigned as homework. However, if at all possible, they should be done in class in pairs. As the students discuss items with each other, they increase their fluency and retention of the idioms. While doing these exercises, students can be referred to the "Put a Fine Point on Them" section at the end of the chapter for more detailed information. A partial ANSWER KEY is provided at the end of the text to help the students, but not to make them lazy.

Get Down to Business/Put It All Together: Each roleplay gives enough details of the situation to allow the students to use all the idioms listed below it. Students can be encouraged to "customize" their roleplays as long as they don't change the plot line (and thus eliminate the need for certain idioms). In many cases, the roleplays encourage customizing. The roleplays also generally allow for a varying number of participants, to accommodate differing class sizes.

To begin, the teacher should assign one roleplay to each student or accept volunteers. Students should then read and discuss their roleplay with their fellow group members. The teacher should provide cards or slips of paper with one idiom from the particular roleplay on each piece or assign students to tear up slips of paper and write one idiom on each piece. Group members should then decide on each other's roles and divide up the slips of paper with the idioms on them. After 6–8 minutes of preparation, performances can begin. If time is short, roleplay preparation can be assigned for out of class.

Each group presents its roleplay for the class. Members may not read anything they have written, but they may hold their idioms (on the slips of paper) in their hands and use them as prompts. The teacher can take notes on any structural or cultural misuses of the idioms for use during debriefing after the roleplays are completed.*

Keep the Ball Rolling: For curricula with unlimited time, this is another small group activity that gives students the opportunity to use the text's idioms. However, when time is limited, these activities should be regarded as a change of pace from the "Put It All Together" roleplays. Students should be divided into groups of three or four and given approximately 15–20 minutes to discuss the topic and prepare its conclusions. In many cases, more than one scenario is given; students should then be encouraged to choose the one that interests them. After the discussion period, one member of the group—chosen by the group or the teacher—should present the group's results to the class, using as many of the idioms listed as possible. The group should help its spokesperson to prepare this part. Again, the teacher can listen for structural or cultural errors in the idioms and discuss them afterward.

Put a Fine Point on Them/Check It Out: Nothing need be done with these sections in class. They exist only for students who need such support.

* For a useful discussion of debriefing, consult Robert J. Di Pietro, *Strategic Interaction*, Cambridge University Press, 1987.

Acknowledgments

Several people deserve mention for their input into this text and their help. First, I would like to thank Christine O'Neill, Allegheny Intermediate Unit, and Joe Sukenik, University of Pittsburgh, for using a number of the chapters in their courses and making valuable suggestions to me. I would also like to thank Carol Jasnow, University of Pittsburgh, for acting as a sounding board and for providing encouragement.

And finally I would like to thank my students for receiving early versions of these chapters good-naturedly and for offering very useful feedback, all the while pretending to believe that I was not really the author.

To the Student

With the help of this text and your instructor, you can learn to speak and understand natural-sounding English. However, to make the best use of this text, there are some things you'll need to know.

First, there is a complete GLOSSARY at the end of the text, which includes definitions and grammatical notes for all of the idioms presented in the text.

There is also a PARTIAL ANSWER KEY at the end of the text to help you while you are doing the "Get Your Bearings" sections in each chapter. This will help you be sure that you are doing the exercise correctly.

Inside each chapter, you'll find complete definitions and examples for the idioms in that chapter in the "Put a Fine Point on Them" section at the end. You can also find the chapter's "Zero In" conversation at the end of the chapter in the "Check It Out" section.

Each section of every chapter is given an idiom title that expresses the instructional intention of that section. Below are the meanings of these idioms:

Get Ready—prepare

Get the Gist—understand the general meaning

Zero In—focus on the most important part

Get Your Bearings—become oriented

Tune In—focus on sound; listen

Get Down to Business—begin the most important work

Put It All Together—combine for complete use

Keep the Ball Rolling—continue the activity

Put a Fine Point on Them—focus on details

Check It Out—look for answers or information

In addition, two abbreviations are used in the definitions:

(Int.)—intransitive

This abbreviation describes verbs that cannot have an object.

For example, the idiom *fall through* cannot have a noun after it.

(S)—separable

Some two-or three-word verbs allow the object to be placed *either* inside the verb phrase *or* after the preposition. However, if the object is a pronoun, it *must* be placed *inside* the verb phrase: check **it** out, check **the facts** out, check out **the facts**.

Time

1

"Time flies when you're having fun."

This expression refers to a common phenomenon. When you're happy, everything seems to happen very fast. But when you're not, time seems to move very slowly. Can you think of some situations when time seems to go too fast or when it "drags"? Do you have an expression like this in your language?

Get Ready

Prepare to hear a conversation by looking at the picture to the left and discussing the questions below with your teacher.

A.

1. What is one young man obviously thinking?
2. Does the other young man seem to agree with him? Can you guess why?

B.

1. Where are the man and woman?
2. What time is it? What do you think they're talking about?
3. Do you think the woman is the man's supervisor? Why or why not?

Get the Gist

Answer these questions after you listen to the conversation one time.

Pizza

1. Do the young men eat pizza often?
2. Why does one man not want to get pizza tonight?
3. Will they have pizza for dinner tonight?

That Terrible Bus

1. Why did Sam miss his bus?
2. Is it unusual for him to be late?
3. Why is it more important than usual for him to be on time now?
4. What does his friend suggest Sam do?
5. What does Sam think about this suggestion?

Zero In

Determine the meanings of this chapter's idioms by listening to the conversation again and circling the most likely meaning for each idiom.

1. *on time*	late	at the correct time	early
2. *ahead of time*	late	at the correct time	early
3. *from now on*	now	often	from this moment
4. *in time*	soon enough	often enough	many times
5. *off and on*	always	sometimes	never
6. *in time*	early	late	eventually
7. *just around the corner*	nearby	soon	not seen
8. *every so often*	sometimes	very often	never
9. *day in and day out*	always	sometimes	never
10. *every now and then*	now	occasionally	in the future
11. *so far*	far away	often	until now
12. *once in a while*	sometimes	always	never
13. *in the long run*	usually	far in the future	soon
14. *for good*	better	now	forever
15. *for the time being*	for a short time	for a long time	in a past time
16. *right away*	correctly	many times	immediately

Get Your Bearings

Use these exercises to become familiar with the idioms. You may want to refer to the definitions and examples at the end of this chapter while you do them.

Exercise 1: Read the first statement, then determine whether the second statement is true (T) or false (F).

1. Because Tom has been having some heart problems, his doctor has told him to stop eating fatty foods from now on.

   _____ Tom will occasionally be permitted to eat fatty foods.

2. Once in a while, I eat far more chocolate than I should.

   _____ I have a continuing problem with chocolate.

3. Jane's cousin arrived unexpectedly and asked to stay at Jane's house. Jane told her cousin she could stay for the time being.

   _____ Jane's cousin will probably not be staying at Jane's home for long.

4. This city gets so cold in the winter and so hot in the summer that I'd like to leave for good.

   _____ I never want to return to this city.

5. Because Rick has gotten poor grades on his last two math tests, his teacher wants to meet with him ahead of time for the next test.

   _____ The math teacher thinks Rick needs help preparing for the test.

6. Nick has sent out hundreds of job applications. His wife said that he's gotten no answers so far.

   _____ Nick's wife thinks he might get answers in the future.

7. That dog barks day in and day out! He's too noisy.

   _____ The dog doesn't bark at night.

8. In time, I'd like to run a small newspaper.

   _____ I expect this to happen soon.

9. With graduation just around the corner, I have to think about getting a job.

   _____ I've already graduated.

10. A friend of mine is living in Egypt. I hear from him off and on.

    _____ He often phones or writes.

Exercise 2: Choose the idiom that best completes the following sentences.

1. Our football team is terrible. _____ it wins, but it usually loses.

   a. Day in and day out
   b. Every so often
   c. From now on

2. Raul: "The rain is coming down hard."
   Julia: "Yes, you closed the window _____."

   a. off and on
   b. every now and then
   c. just in time

3. Be sure to get here _____. We want to begin promptly at 6:00.

   a. on time
   b. in the long run
   c. so far

4. I've decided to stop taking airplanes _____. After that terrible accident, I never want to take any more risks.

    a. for good
    b. once in a while
    c. in time

5. Bill came home 2 hours late last night. His parents told him to come home earlier _____.

    a. just around the corner
    b. so far
    c. from now on

6. Everybody's excited because Thanksgiving* is _____. It's time to plan for it.

    a. ahead of time
    b. just around the corner
    c. off and on

7. We were just a little surprised to lose our electricity during the storm. That happens _____.

    a. day in and day out
    b. off and on
    c. right away

8. "The papers are on fire! Throw some water on them _____!"

    a. every now and then
    b. once in a while
    c. right away

9. I want to be a lawyer, but I'm also studying medicine. _____ I'd like to work in health law.

    a. for the time being
    b. off and on
    c. in the long run

10. Pete doesn't believe in studying foreign languages in a classroom. He thinks if he lives in another culture long enough, he will learn its language _____.

    a. on time
    b. in time
    c. ahead of time

Exercise 3: In the U.S., it's very popular for people (especially business people) to have "frequent flier cards." People who travel a lot have frequent flier accounts with a particular airline. Whenever they fly with that airline, the distance of the flight is recorded in their account. After they accumulate a certain number of miles, they are eligible for discounted or free trips, hotel rooms, and car rentals.

---

* A U.S. holiday to give thanks for health and happiness.

In the following sentences about frequent flier accounts, determine whether the underlined idiom can be substituted for the idiom in parentheses at the end of the sentence *without changing the meaning*. Write Y for *yes* and N for *no*.

1. _____ Even if you only fly <u>every now and then</u>, it's a good idea to have a frequent flier account.
(off and on)

2. _____ This is because, <u>in time</u>, you can accumulate enough miles for a frequent flier award even if you don't travel often.
(on time)

3. _____ For example, a flier who has traveled 20,000 miles with one airline <u>so far</u> is eligible for a 25% discount with one airline.
(for good)

4. _____ Airlines offer frequent flier accounts because, <u>in the long run</u>, they will attract more customers that way.
(for the time being)

5. _____ For example, there are many people who don't care which airline they fly with. They might fly with one particular airline only <u>once in a while</u>.
(every so often)

6. _____ But if they have a frequent flier account with a particular airline, they will probably stay with that airline <u>for good</u>.
(from now on)

7. _____ <u>For the time being</u>, frequent flier accounts seem to be more popular with business travelers than general travelers.
(in the long run)

8. _____ There are, of course, some inconveniences with frequent flier accounts. First, the airline must have your account number when you board the airplane. Sometimes, this is difficult if you are not <u>on time</u> for your flight.
(right away)

9. _____ You have to be careful to give your account number <u>ahead of time</u>, either to the airline ticket agent or your travel agent.
(off and on)

10. _____ Second, businesses don't always like their employees to use frequent flier accounts because the employees travel with the same airline <u>day in and day out</u>, without paying attention to the prices of that airline compared with other airlines.
(for good)

11. _____ In general, however, frequent flier accounts are a bonus for the traveler. If you travel by airplane, your free trip could be <u>just around the corner</u>, with a frequent flier card in your hands.
(ahead of time)

12. _____ <u>In time</u>, you could accumulate enough miles for a trip around the world, paid for by the airline!
(in the long run)

Tune In   Improve your ability to hear and understand idioms by listening to several statements, then read the question and circle the letter of the correct answer.

1. When did Jack plan to get to work?

    a. a little late
    b. earlier than usual
    c. exactly on time

2. What can we understand from this requirement?

    a. People don't want to waste time waiting for late planes.
    b. People want cheaper airline tickets.
    c. The government is trying to protect the airline companies.

3. What career does the speaker want?

    a. computer science
    b. computer science and math
    c. She/he hasn't made a decision yet.

4. What does the speaker think about computer science and engineering?

    a. Computer science is a good career now, but engineering will be better in the future.
    b. Computer science and engineering are probably equally good careers.
    c. Engineering is good now, but computer science will be a better career in the future.

5. Why has Sara stopped talking to her husband?

    a. Because it is good.
    b. Because he is good.
    c. We don't know.

6. When does the phone ring?

    a. very often
    b. once in while
    c. every night

7. What do we know from this statement?

    a. We know where his graduation will be.
    b. We know his graduation will be soon.
    c. We know what kind of gift he wants.

8. What is Dr. Michaels probably going to do next?

    a. see another patient
    b. go home
    c. fly to a medical conference

9. How often does the speaker fly in airplanes?

    a. almost never
    b. very often
    c. sometimes

10. When does Chris cook?

    a. during the day
    b. all the time
    c. occasionally

Get Down to Business

Improve your ability to use this chapter's idioms in conversation with a couple of your classmates by acting out one or more of the roleplays below.

1. (2–3 friends)

Both/All of you have different ideas about time. One of you is always late; the second is always very early (the third is always exactly on time). These different ideas always cause trouble when you are having parties or meeting to go out. Tonight is the "last straw."* Everybody arrived at the "wrong" time to go to dinner and nobody is happy. This might be the end of the friendship!

Argue about this situation using the following idioms:

so far	**ahead of time**	**from now on**
on time	**for good**	**in time**
every now and then	**once in a while**	**day in and day out**

2. (a teacher and a student)

There was a big test today. You missed the test because your car broke down on the highway. You must now convince the teacher that you tried to come to the test but couldn't. You want the teacher to allow you to take the test now. The teacher is not very willing to give you another chance at first.

Discuss this situation using the following idioms:

ahead of time	**from now on**	**in time**
so far	**for the time being**	**for good**
	once in a while	

3. (a man and a woman)

You are planning to get married and you must "set the date" for the wedding. The problem is that there are a lot of holidays coming soon. You need enough time to

---

* An additional problem that causes one finally to lose one's patience.

plan, and, besides, you want to pick a day that will give you a beautiful anniversary. You have a lot of dates that are possible, but you can't choose just one.

Discuss your decision using the following idioms:

in the long run	**just around the corner**	**in time**
once in a while	**for the time being**	**so far**
right away	**ahead of time**	

4. (an airline employee and a passenger)

You are planning to take a trip to (you decide where). You've arrived at the airport 15 minutes ahead of time, and you discover that your seat has been given to someone else. Airlines in the U.S. require passengers to arrive 20 minutes ahead of time or possibly lose their seats. You are very angry and try to discuss the matter with the airline employee.

Use the following idioms in your discussion:

ahead of time	**once in a while**	**every so often**
in the long run	**right away**	**on time**
for good	**for the time being**	

Keep the Ball Rolling

Get still more practice with the idioms you've learned so far by participating in a discussion.

1. Each culture has its own perception of time—what's late, what's early, what's on time. The following situations illustrate some information about the U.S. sense of time. Read them and discuss with a couple of your classmates what the U.S. "rules" for time are likely to be and compare them with the "rules" in your country. Use the idioms below in your discussion of these "rules." Based on these situations, what recommendations can you give someone who is planning a trip to the U.S.?*

A. Joanna and her husband have invited several friends for dinner at a restaurant tonight at 8:00. It's now 8:15, and Joanna is upset because nobody has arrived yet. She wonders whether nobody will come or whether they've had a car accident.

B. Tom and his wife have invited a couple to their home for dinner tonight at 8:00. It's 7:45 and Tom is making a special sauce for the main course. Suddenly their doorbell rings. It's clear that the guests have arrived. Tom is very upset because he hasn't had time to finish preparing the meal. In his mind, he promises never to invite these rude people again.

C. Cathy just got a telephone call from a co-worker who wants to invite Cathy and her husband to a dinner party the following night. Even though Cathy is free, she

---

* See page 227 for possible solutions.

declines the invitation. After she hangs up, she tells her husband how angry she is. Cathy believes that her co-worker only invited her because one of the original guests canceled at the last minute.

D. Francisco's boss told him yesterday that Francisco wasn't working hard enough—even though he works more hours a day than anyone else in the company. Francisco has noticed that his co-workers rarely sit at their desks.

E. Nano doesn't understand Americans. Whenever he sees someone he knows, he wants to stop and talk with them, to be polite. But these people just say "Hi" and keep walking. Sometimes he asks Americans, "How are you?" and they answer "Busy, busy," without stopping to talk. And when he finally does manage to find Americans to talk to for a few minutes, he usually can't say much to them because they always finish his sentences for him.

Use these idioms in your analysis of each situation above:

every now and then	**once in a while**	**on time**
ahead of time	**in time**	**off and on**
every so often	**day in and day out**	**from now on**
for the time being	**right away**	**in the long run**
for good		

Put a Fine Point on Them

Use the following definitions and examples to help you understand the details of this chapter's idioms when you do the exercises.

1. *every now and then*—sometimes; not often (compare with *every so often* and *once in a while*)

   Every now and then, my boss checks to see if I'm working or sleeping.
   We have terrible thunderstorms every now and then.

2. *day in and day out*—always; continually

   Many diabetics must take insulin day in and day out.
   Day in and day out, the flag flies above the White House.

3. *every so often*—sometimes; not often (compare with *every now and then* and *once in a while*)

   Every so often, I like a nice cup of hot chocolate with whipped cream.
   There's a traffic accident in that intersection every so often.

4. *for good*—forever (used especially with verbs meaning "finishing")

   Joe said he's left the rural life for good because he was bored with it.
   Billie stopped writing songs for good. She says she's lost the creative urge.

5. *for the time being*—currently; for a short time; now

   I'm only studying English for the time being. I actually plan to study engineering after this.
   For the time being, let's stay in this apartment. It's convenient enough.

6. *off and on*—sometimes; not often (used especially for actions that stop and start again)

> I've studied music off and on all my life.
> Bob's not a serious student. He just takes courses off and on.

7. *once in a while*—sometimes; not often (compare with *every now and then* and *every so often*)

> Once in a while, our neighbors get very noisy.
> I saw Barb downtown once in a while during the summer.

8. *right away*—immediately

> Call the paramedics right away. Tony's unconscious.
> My watch was missing. Right away, Bill said somebody probably stole it.

9. *just around the corner*—soon; an event very near in time

> Our vacation is just around the corner. Are you going to do anything special?
> My final exam is just around the corner, so I have to study all week.

10. *in time*—a) eventually, after some time

> In time, I hope to get my Ph.D.
> My son and daughter-in-law will work out their problems in time.

   b) soon enough (+ to + V) (often used with *just* for emphasis)

> Did you get to the concert in time to hear the soloist?
> We arrived at the stadium just in time to see our team score the winning point.

11. *on time*—at the correct time

> Our teacher gets angry if we don't come to class on time.
> Physicians rarely start appointments on time.

12. *so far*—until now (uses present perfect or past perfect verb forms)

> How many college credits have you earned so far?
> So far, I've never owned a car.

13. *in the long run*—in the end; far into the future; eventually

> In the long run, what you eat has a strong effect on your health.
> Long hours of study now will make you more successful in the long run.

14. *ahead of time*—early; before the scheduled time (appears only at the end of a clause or sentence)

> I missed my flight because it left ahead of time.
> I like to do my homework ahead of time, so I can have the weekend free.

15. *from now on*—from this moment, beginning now and continuing forever

> I'm going to stop eating red meat from now on.
> From now on, you'll have to take the bus.

Check It Out

Take a closer look at the conversation from the "Zero In" section if you want to see any words or phrases that you might not have understood.

Pizza

Bob: What's for dinner?

Ben: Let's get a pizza.

Bob: We just had one yesterday. We can't eat pizza **day in and day out.**

Ben: We don't eat pizza all the time. We've only had two **so far** this week.

Bob: Look, eating a pizza **every now and then,** maybe once a month or two, is OK. But it's not good for our health if we eat it all the time. **In the long run,** we'll be healthier when we're old if we stop eating so many pizzas now.

Ben: Are you suggesting that we stop eating pizza forever? Can you really quit eating pizza **for good?** No more tomato sauce, cheese, pepperoni for the rest of your life?

Bob: Uh . . . I don't think I said that, exactly. But since we've already had two this week, **for the time being** we shouldn't have another one. That's all I meant. We'll just wait a little bit.

Ben: Hot, spicy sauce . . . melted mozzarella cheese . . . crispy crust . . .

Bob: Stop it. You're making me hungry . . . OK. OK. Let's go.

Ben: Really?

Bob: Yes. But immediately. We'll have to go **right away,** before I reconsider.

That Terrible Bus

Kathy: Sam, you're really late. You've been late three times this week.

Sam: I know. But it's not my fault.

Kathy: Why aren't you **on time** this morning?

Sam: It's my bus. I missed it. I think the bus arrived **ahead of time.** I thought I was 5 minutes early.

Kathy: **From now on,** you should leave your house **in time** to catch your bus.

Sam: Yeah, I know. You're right.

Kathy: It might even be nice if you arrived early **off and on.** Maybe not every day, but you should get to work on time occasionally.

Sam: I know that. I don't *try* to be late.

Kathy: I know that, but I heard that **in time,** after you get more experience, you're expected to take a lot of responsibility in this company. Decisions on promotions are **just around the corner,** maybe even next month. I just want you to get a good recommendation.

Sam: So do I. But **every so often,** I wonder whether I'll ever be promoted.

Kathy: Sure you will. But maybe you should buy a car, just to be sure.

Sam: I'm not so sure that I want a car. It's really a problem finding a place to park **day in and day out.**

Kathy: That's true. **So far** this week, I've only been able to park my car by the stadium. That's a pretty long walk every morning and afternoon.

Sam: Yeah, but it isn't only that. Parking a car is a lot more expensive than riding a bus. **In the long run,** I'm probably going to save enough money to buy a house.

Kathy: Ha, ha. I'm not sure about *that*. Well, maybe a small one.

Sam: No, I mean it. The more I think about it, the smarter it seems to continue taking the bus **for good.** It will always be a better deal than a car.

Kathy: Well, maybe it seems like a good idea **for the time being,** but you're going to have to think about your professional future too. If you continue to come to work late, you'll wish you'd gotten a car **right away** instead of waiting.

Plans and Schedules

2

"Better late than never!"

This means that it's better to arrive someplace late than never to arrive at all. Do you agree? Do you know an expression like this in your language? When might you say this to someone? Is it polite?

Get Ready

Prepare to hear a conversation by looking at the picture to the left and discussing the questions below with your teacher.

1. What is the woman holding in her hand? What does it mean?
2. Does the man look happy?
3. Can you guess what the woman might be telling the man?

Get the Gist

Answer these questions after you listen to the conversation one time.

Problem Graduation

1. Why can't Patty graduate on time?
2. How do her friends plan to help her?
3. What is cheating? Why are her friends worried about it?

Zero In

Determine the meanings of this chapter's idioms by listening to the conversation again and circling the most likely meaning for each idiom.

1. *be about to*	be ready	be nearby	be around
2. *keep track of*	find	remember	understand
3. *look forward to*	watch carefully	dislike	happily expect
4. *call off*	telephone	cancel	remove
5. *fall through*	fail to happen	come down	descend
6. *fall behind*	drop	forget	go too slowly

7. *catch up on*	find	agree with the schedule	take
8. *put off*	make later	create	schedule
9. *on the spur of the moment*	for a long time	with strong attention	without planning
10. *behind schedule*	early	on time	late
11. *around the clock*	continuously	with a clock	at certain times
12. *make good time*	waste time	work fast	spend a lot of time
13. *carry out*	hold	avoid	complete
14. *bring up to date*	write the date	cause to agree with the schedule	discover the time
15. *move back*	schedule later	change the location	schedule earlier
16. *move up*	lift	schedule earlier	change the location

Get Your Bearings

Use these exercises to become familiar with the idioms. You may want to refer to the definitions and examples at the end of this chapter while you do them.

Exercise 1: Read each statement and write T for true or F for false.

_____ *1.* People who make good time are usually late.

_____ *2.* If your plans for tonight fall through, you may have to stay home.

_____ *3.* When someone is about to retire, he doesn't have a job now.

_____ *4.* Doctors shouldn't recommend serious operations on the spur of the moment.

_____ *5.* When you are behind schedule, you have to hurry.

_____ *6.* People are usually afraid of things that they look forward to.

_____ *7.* People who are on diets should keep track of the food they eat.

_____ *8.* When you need more time to finish something, you move up the date that it's due.

_____ *9.* If your friends call off their party, you'll probably be disappointed.

_____ *10.* In order to catch up on something, you have to work extra hard.

_____ *11.* Bringing my appointment book up to date means that I count my appointments.

_____ *12.* Most people like to work around the clock.

_____ *13.* It's a good idea to fall behind often.

_____ *14.* When a bride calls off the wedding, the groom* won't be happy.

_____ *15.* When a bride and groom are not sure about getting married, it's a good idea for them to put the wedding off until they decide.

Exercise 2: Choose the one subject or object that can be used in each sentence below.

1. It's extremely important to keep track of _____.

   a. your money
   b. bad memories
   c. all of the programs on TV

2. I was happy when _____ was called off.

   a. the midterm examination
   b. the airplane
   c. my birthday

3. I would like to move _____ up.

   a. my apartment
   b. his sickness
   c. my dentist appointment

4. I can't go with you. I have to catch up on _____.

   a. my homework
   b. the children
   c. a cold

5. _____ made good time.

   a. The clock
   b. The schedule
   c. The bus

6. The president is looking forward to _____.

   a. losing the next election
   b. meeting with the leaders of other countries
   c. being assassinated

7. Secretaries have to carry _____ out.

   a. the garbage
   b. their bosses' instructions
   c. their children

8. The _____ operates around the clock.

   a. university class
   b. symphony
   c. fire department

* The man who is going to get married.

9. Joe put off _____.

    a. his wedding anniversary
    b. a car accident
    c. the meeting

10. We don't want _____ to fall through.

    a. the picnic
    b. the family
    c. the airplane

Exercise 3: Jasper is not an efficient assistant manager, but he keeps his job because his uncle owns the company. The manager was on vacation for 2 weeks, and now Jasper must write a report about what happened while the manager was gone. Fill in the blanks with an idiom from this list below to complete Jasper's report.

fell through	**keep track of**	**making good time**
bring you up to date	**carry out**	**behind schedule**
called off	**am about to**	**put off**
around the clock	**catch up**	**looking forward to**
move up	**on the spur of the moment**	

Report on the Past Three Weeks

    This report should _____ on all our projects and employee situations. I hope you understand everything here because my wife invited me to

Hawaii _____ , so I won't be here the rest of this month. (She loves to surprise me with these little trips!)

1. The deal with the Corona Corporation _____. They no longer want us to build their new skyscraper. This may be my fault. I told them most of us are afraid of heights. It was just a joke! They're awfully sensitive, aren't they?

2. I can't remember how many people started their vacations last week. I started

    to _____ this in my special little notebook, but I lost it. Sorry. My fault.

3. For the first few days after you left, we were _____ on the Randall project. There were no problems and everything was proceeding well. But everybody was getting tired, so I gave all of them an extra week's vaca-

    tion. Now we're _____. But don't worry. Everyone can

    work _____ until we're on schedule again. I think it'll take

    about 6 weeks to _____. (That's because everyone went on strike when they discovered they would have to work 24 hours a day.)

4. I had to _____ the Gleason project for a few months. They wanted us to begin next month, but since we're already behind schedule on

the Randall project, I had to tell them to wait. Besides, I'll be on vacation for

a month, so I won't be able to _____ the project. I know that you always like me to be involved in the projects personally.

5. I got a lot of telephone calls about your daughter's wedding plans. Frankly, I didn't have time to answer all these questions (I was so busy thinking about my vacation), so I finally told everyone that your daughter's wedding was

_____. (In my opinion, he's not the right man for her anyway.) You might want to tell her about this.

6. Finally, I did something that will make you very happy. I asked the President

of the company (my uncle) to _____ your retirement date. I know you don't really like coming to work, and I feel ready to take your

place sooner than I expected. Besides, I'm sure you are _____ the day when you won't have to come to work. No! Don't thank me. Your happiness will be thanks enough.

Well, now that I've written this report, I _____ go home. I need to plan for my vacation. Welcome back!

Tune In

Improve your ability to hear and understand idioms by listening to several statements and answering the questions below T for True or F for False.

1. _____ The speaker likes going to these lectures.

2. _____ The speaker was angry because the bus came late.

3. _____ The workers will be working very hard.

4. _____ Kathy's airplane arrived earlier than we expected.

5. _____ Steve plans to go to technical school because it won't take as much time as college.

6. _____ The police may not support the new law.

7. _____ We should make our appointment a little earlier.

8. _____ We can go to the rock concert if more people buy tickets soon.

9. _____ Medical students have to keep samples of many different drugs.

10. _____ I had to get out of bed to answer the phone.

Get Down to Business

Improve your ability to use this chapter's idioms in conversation with a couple of your classmates by acting out one or more of the roleplays below.

1. (2–3 people)

You are traveling to a friend's home in another part of the country. You haven't seen your friend in more than a year. You had expected to have a lot of extra time, but, because you started your trip late and you've had some trouble following the map, you will probably arrive at your friend's house a day late. You are discussing how to handle the problem. There are several possibilities: not stopping to eat, driving all night, canceling the visit. You blame each other for the problem.

Use the following idioms in your conversation:

look forward to	**make good time**	**behind schedule**
ahead of schedule	**call off**	**fall behind**
around the clock	**keep track of**	**fall through**
	put off	

2. (a mother and daughter OR a father and son)

Your child is planning to get married, but now that the wedding is only a week away, he or she is getting "cold feet."* He/she has been very nervous all the time about the marriage and the new husband/wife, but also about the ceremony and all the plans that are necessary for a big wedding. You are trying to convince your child that everyone gets cold feet before a wedding.

Use the following idioms in your discussion:

be about to	**fall through**	**keep track of**
look forward to	**behind schedule**	**move back**
put off	**call off**	**carry out**
on the spur of the moment	**around the clock**	**just around the corner**

3. (2–3 students)

Three students who are friends are talking about the end of the semester, which is coming soon. One of the friends is very worried about finishing his/her work on time. Two friends offer suggestions for how to finish on time, including working hard, talking to the teacher, and asking for extra time.

Use the following idioms in your discussion:

keep track of	**make good time**	**behind schedule**
move back	**bring up to date**	**carry out**
fall behind	**around the clock**	**catch up on**

4. (a husband, wife, and construction contractor)

You bought a house 6 months ago for a very low price because it needed a lot of construction work. It was supposed to be ready by next week, but it's clear that there's still a lot of work to be done before you can move into it. The contractor gives a lot of reasons for the slow work: some materials are hard to find, the workers keep getting sick, the house is a lot harder to work on than predicted. You are getting very angry about this. You want to move into your house soon.

* "Get cold feet" means become afraid.

Use the following idioms in your discussion:

be about to	**fall through**	**keep track of**
look forward to	**(not) make good time**	**behind schedule**
move back	**around the clock**	**put off**
carry out	**fall behind**	**catch up on**

Put It All Together

Reinforce your ability to speak using many of the idioms you've learned so far by acting out one or more of the roleplays below with your classmates.

1. (2 applicants at the department of transportation)

One of the applicants has been waiting in line for almost 40 minutes to apply for a driver's license. The clerk will handle this person's application next. Suddenly a second applicant hurries in. He asks the first applicant to allow him to go first because he is in a big hurry. He has tickets to the baseball game, which starts in 30 minutes. The first applicant is not happy about this because he is tired and wants to go home to dinner, but the second applicant is persistent. They discuss it and argue a little.

Use the following idioms in your discussion:

be about to	**fall behind**	**behind schedule**
right away	**ahead of time**	**in time**
look forward to	**on time**	**so far**
	make good time	

2. (a job applicant and two employers)

You are interviewing an applicant for a job that requires a lot of hard work. You are trying to be sure that the applicant knows how to work efficiently and is willing to work hard. The person who had the job previously could never stay on schedule. The applicant makes a lot of promises about working long hours and good planning because he or she really wants the job.

Use the following idioms in your discussion:

keep track of	**look forward to**	**fall behind**
catch up on	**behind schedule**	**around the clock**
carry out	**bring up to date**	**day in and day out**
in the long run	**once in a while**	**right away**
from now on	**on time**	

3. (a dental patient and the dentist's nurse, on the telephone)

You're very nervous about seeing your dentist tomorrow. Ever since you were a child, dentists have meant pain for you. After a particularly bad nightmare last night, you've decided to postpone your visit, maybe even cancel it (although you won't tell the nurse the truth). You are telephoning the dentist's office to do this. However, the dentist's nurse knows your history of fear (you've done this many times before) and tries to convince you to come tomorrow. Dentistry is no longer painful!

Use the following idioms in your discussion:

be about to	**behind schedule**	**move back**
put off	**call off**	**catch up on**
on the spur of the moment	**look forward to**	**so far**
	from now on	**for the time being**
in the long run		

4. (1 or 2 parents and a teacher)

You've moved from another country and put your 7-year-old child into school recently. You are at the school now to discuss your child's progress with the teacher. You are worried that the different culture and language might be interfering with your child's education. The teacher feels the child is making slow progress now because of the language differences, but will do better in the future. Your child usually has normal relations with the other children. The teacher has plans for helping your child.

Use the following idioms in your conversation:

keep track of	**make good time**	**behind schedule**
catch up	**bring up to date**	**in time**
every so often	**so far**	**from now on**
carry out	**in the long run**	**look forward to**

Keep the Ball Rolling   Get still more practice with the idioms you've learned so far by participating in a discussion.

Choose one of the following topics to discuss with some of your classmates.

1. Ken is about to become a physician in the U.S., and he's getting ready to establish an office in his town. He's been trying to plan how his nurse should schedule appointments. A couple of friends who have been physicians for several years have told him that he should schedule each appointment only 15 minutes apart because so many patients don't come for their appointments. Besides, they tell him, most patients don't require a lot of the doctor's time. However, Ken remembers how angry his mother and other family members used to be when

they had to wait nearly an hour to see their doctors even though they already had appointments.

How can Ken maximize his efficiency while being fair to his patients?

Use the following idioms in your discussion:

keep track of	**fall behind**	**catch up on**
put off	**behind schedule**	**make good time**
every now and then	**in the long run**	**right away**
on time	**ahead of time**	**every so often**
move back	**move up**	

2. Pat and Cindy, sisters who live together, are planning to visit their family in another city during the spring vacation. They haven't seen their family for several months and are excited. Their family is planning a big welcome home party for them with all the relatives and friends as soon as they arrive. But when Pat and Cindy arrive at the airport, they are told that their flight has been canceled because there weren't enough seats sold. The airline will give them a seat on the next flight, 6 hours from now. Pat and Cindy are determined to get to their family's home in time for the party.

What can they do? Do you think the airline is being fair? If you were writing a law to cover this problem, what would you say?

Use the following idioms in your discussion:

about to	**look forward to**	**call off**
fall through	**put off**	**on the spur of the moment**
behind schedule	**move back**	
from now on	**every now and then**	**off and on**
for the time being	**right away**	

Put a Fine Point on Them

Use the following definitions and examples to help you understand the details of this chapter's idioms when you do the exercises.

1. *be about to*—be almost ready to; be close to doing something (+ V)

   I was about to buy that yellow dress when I noticed a hole in its sleeve.
   You're late. I was about to leave.

2. *fall through*—(Int.) fail to happen or be completed against one's will (only takes inanimate subjects)

   Our picnic will fall through if it rains.
   The president's schedule fell through when his plane arrived late.

3. *keep track of*—maintain a written or mental record of; remember

   Secretaries have to keep track of their bosses' appointments.
   It's hard for dieters to keep track of how many calories they consume.

4. *look forward to*—happily expect (+ Verb + ing or + Noun)

> High school students look forward to their graduation day.
> John really looked forward to having his first child.

5. *make good time*—finish faster than usual or than expected (+ V + ing)

> I thought this homework would take all night. We really made good time doing it.
> Our airplane may arrive late, but we'll make good time because the weather is very good.

6. *behind schedule*—later than planned

> Because the speaker was behind schedule, the next lecture began late too.
> Physicians are often behind schedule, so patients have to wait for them.

7. *move up*—(S) schedule for an earlier time

> Can you move my appointment up an hour, from 2:00 to 1:00?
> The conference was moved up 1 week because the election was at the same time.

8. *move back*—(S) schedule for a later time

> My car broke down. Can you move our meeting back an hour?
> The lecture was moved back a month to allow more time for advance publicity.

9. *put off*—(S) postpone; schedule for a later time (+ N; + Verb + ing)

> My brother had to put off graduating because he failed a course.
> Let's put the purchase of a car off until we can get more information.

10. *call off*—(S) cancel, cause not to happen (+N; + Verb + ing)

> Richard was so nervous that he almost called his wedding off.
> The president called off going to the city after she received a death threat.

11. *bring up to date*—(S) modernize; give all current information

> The medical records must be brought up to date.
> The publishers brought the dictionary up to date to include more technical words.

12. *carry out*—(S) fulfill a process; complete

> In order to carry out our plans, we'll need to do some research.
> Soldiers must carry their superiors' orders out.

13. *on the spur of the moment*—without planning or careful thought; impulsively

> On the spur of the moment, the visiting president stepped out of his car to talk to the people.
> Mrs. Fulton accepted a kitten from her neighbor on the spur of the moment because she was lonely in her big house.

14. *fall behind (on something)* (Int.)—to be slower than the schedule requires

> I fell behind on my homework. Now I have to work twice as hard.
> The workers fell behind, so the house isn't ready yet.

15. *around the clock*—24 hours each day; continuously

> Many convenience stores are open around the clock.
> Would you like English classes around the clock?

16. *catch up (on something)*—try to be on schedule after going too slowly

> I have to catch up on my laundry, or I'll have nothing to wear tomorrow.
> Joyce stayed up late last night to catch up on some paperwork.

Check It Out

Take a closer look at the conversation from the "Zero In" section if you want to see any words or phrases that you might not have understood.

Problem Graduation

Abby: Did you hear about Patty? She's **about to** leave school.

Ken: She is? Why? She's such a good student.

Abby: She's failing her history class.

Ken: What happened?

Abby: She says she can't **keep track of** all the dates and names.

Ken: That's true. It's awfully hard to remember all of them.

Abby: Her family was really **looking forward to** her graduating. You know, she was the first person in her family to go to college, and they were very excited.

Ken: That's such a pity. I know her family was planning a graduation party for her. I guess they'll have to **call off** the party.

Abby: Yes, that's clear, since Pat's plans to graduate have **fallen through**. No graduation, no party.

Ken: I'm not sure I understand why she's leaving, though.

Abby: Well, she **fell behind** in all her work. She owes two research papers. Remember, she was sick a month ago? Since then, she hasn't been able to **catch up on** her work, even though she's been working hard.

Ken: I forgot about that. I feel so sorry for her. She must be upset that she has to **put off** her graduation and graduate later than everyone else. But did she think about this decision carefully or did she decide **on the spur of the moment**?

Abby: I'm sure she thought about it a lot, but she's too far **behind schedule**. She has too much work to do. I mean, the only way she could graduate now is if she studies **around the clock**, all day, every day, until graduation day.

Ken: Can we help her?

Abby: I don't know. What do you think?

Ken: Well, I think if we all work together we can **make good time**. We can get the work done a lot faster.

Abby: But isn't that cheating? I don't want to do anything against the rules.

Ken: No, we'll only help her. Pat will have to **carry out** the actual writing and take the tests. We'll just organize notes and find books and articles for her.

Abby: That's a good idea. With all of us working together, Pat can **bring** her work **up to date**, and then she can graduate on time.

Ken: Great! Do you think she'll like our plan?

Abby: What choice does she have? The school isn't going to **move** graduation **back** a month to June instead of May. . . . Together the three of us can **move** Pat's work schedule **up** instead.

Cooperation

3

"You scratch my back, and I'll scratch yours."

This expression is about cooperation. If you do something for me, then I'll do something for you. Do you have an expression like this in your language? In your culture, is it common for people to "do a favor" for someone only if he does one first? When might you say this?

Get Ready

Prepare to hear a conversation by looking at the picture to the left and discussing the questions below with your teacher.

A.

1. Do these people look angry with each other?
2. Where are they?
3. What do you think they are discussing?

B.

1. What is one of the young men holding?
2. What do you think the two men are discussing?
3. Do they seem to agree with each other?

Get the Gist

Answer these questions after you listen to the conversation one time.

A New Job

1. Why is the woman accepting another job?
2. Where did the woman get most of her job experience?
3. Is her boss angry that she's leaving? How do you know?

A Great Apartment

1. Where does one speaker suggest that the other can find an apartment?
2. What are some reasons he gives for why it's a good place to live?
3. Why does the other speaker disagree?

Zero In

Determine the meanings of this chapter's idioms by listening to the conversation again and circling the most likely meaning for each idiom.

A New Job

1. *right-hand woman* — secretary — most helpful assistant — wife
2. *hand in hand* — holding hands — shaking hands — together
3. *given me a hand* — helped — hit — written a letter
4. *meet each other halfway* — travel — cooperate — introduce each other
5. *came through for* — solved a need — arrived in time — traveled together
6. *gave me my first break* — broke something — promised — gave a chance
7. *bend over backwards to* — show respect — try very hard — start again
8. *do you a favor* — like better — do a kindness — taste something

A Great Apartment

9. *take turns* — alternate — move in a circle — spin
10. *pull together* — work hard — attach — help each other
11. *give and take* — cooperation — jealousy — selling and buying
12. *helping (me) out* — taking away — removing — assisting
13. *see eye to eye* — agree — stand together — look at each other
14. *back me up* — walk behind me — support me — return to me
15. *keep (his) word* — fulfill a promise — be quiet — listen to a secret

Get Your Bearings

Use these exercises to become familiar with the idioms. You may want to refer to the definitions and examples at the end of this chapter while you do them.

Exercise 1: Read each statement and write T for true and F for false.

_____ 1. It's a bad idea for government negotiators to meet each other halfway.

_____ 2. If I couldn't pay my rent this month, I might ask my landlord to give me a break.

_____ 3. When two children are sharing one toy, they might have to take turns playing with it.

_____ 4. The vice president of a country should try hard not to back up the president.

_____ 5. You shouldn't talk to people who do favors for other people.

_____ 6. Parents often come though for their children.

_____ 7. Everybody likes a boss who doesn't keep her word.

_____ 8. Right-hand men always write with their right hands.

_____ 9. You should bend over backwards to help a good friend in trouble.

_____ 10. People who don't see eye to eye work well together.

_____ 11. People who do things hand in hand have to be in love with each other.

_____ 12. Parents should try to teach their children about give and take.

_____ 13. You have to be very athletic to bend over backwards to help someone.

_____ 14. I should be disappointed in someone who gives me a hand.

_____ 15. I should thank someone who helps me out.

Exercise 2: Choose the most appropriate idiom for each sentence.

1. Every U.S. president has a chief of staff, a _____ who helps the president with all aspects of national business.

    _a._ give and take
    _b._ right-hand man or woman
    _c._ hand in hand

2. I was going to miss an important meeting because my car wouldn't start. But my neighbor _____. She drove me to work.

    _a._ came through for me
    _b._ pulled together
    _c._ met me halfway

3. I can't live with my roommate any longer because we never _____. We always argue about food, money, and visitors.

    _a._ keep our word
    _b._ bend over backwards
    _c._ see eye to eye

4. I was sick the night before our history test, and I couldn't study. I asked the teacher to _____. He's going to let me take a different test on Monday.

    _a._ give me a break
    _b._ keep his word
    _c._ take turns

5. A homeless man downtown asked me, "Can you ____?" I gave him a few dollars.

   a. help me out
   b. pull together
   c. bend over backwards

6. Would you ____? Hold the door open for me while I carry in these books.

   a. back me up
   b. give me a break
   c. give me a hand

7. Bill, I need you to ____. Answer the phone and tell whoever it is that I'm not home.

   a. take turns
   b. do me a favor
   c. see eye to eye with me

8. New businesses were brought into the city because the government, existing businesses, and neighborhood people ____ and created a strong plan.

   a. took turns
   b. had a right-hand woman
   c. pulled together

9. We want the city to lower taxes. The mayor will listen if you ____. He respects your opinion.

   a. back us up
   b. meet us halfway
   c. give us a break

10. Dan told me I could visit him in Hawaii and stay with him anytime I wanted to. He ____. I went last month, and he treated me very well.

    a. gave me a hand
    b. kept his word
    c. bent over backwards

11. Successful negotiators use ____ to solve problems. They understand that they can't get everything they want.

    a. give and take
    b. hand in hand
    c. take turns

12. We tried to convince our teacher to stop giving us homework, but he wouldn't even ____.

    a. pull together
    b. meet us halfway
    c. take turns

Exercise 3: You are a radio news writer for an all-news station that is in the middle of a campaign to increase its audience. This afternoon, you wrote a story about a group of neighbors who are trying to prevent a new prison from being built near their neighborhood. Your editor has returned the story to you because it's "flat" and told you to "zip it up" (make it more exciting). She underlined the "boring" phrases for you to change.

Replace the underlined phrases with more vivid language from the list below.

keep her word	**backed up**	**took turns**
bend over backwards	**help them out**	**meet them halfway**
see eye to eye	**hand in hand**	**right-hand man**
come through for them	**pull together**	

Residents of the Marvin Park area held a demonstration outside Mayor Williams' office today. They <u>alternated with each other in</u> accusing the mayor of being unwilling to <u>compromise</u> on the location of the new Hammond Prison facility.

Last month, the mayor, <u>supported</u> by City Council, contracted to build a prison annex 2 miles outside of Marvin Park. Since then, Marvin Park residents have been working <u>together</u> to change its location, but they say that the mayor has been completely unwilling to <u>assist them</u>.

The mayor's <u>executive assistant</u> denies this, saying the mayor has been <u>trying extremely hard</u> to find a solution to the problem. But he admits that the residents and mayor will probably never <u>agree with each other</u>.

Eight months ago, Superior Court ruled that existing prisons were overcrowded and ordered construction of six new prisons in the state. At that time, the mayor promised not to allow any prisons near city neighborhoods. However, financial considerations stopped her from <u>fulfilling that promise</u>. Marvin Park residents are determined to <u>work with each other</u> until the mayor <u>satisfies their demands</u>.

Tune In

Improve your ability to hear and understand idioms by listening to several statements and answering the questions below T for True or F for False.

1. _____ It seems that the speaker will get the job.
2. _____ The speaker's best friend sometimes gets tickets to the basketball games.
3. _____ Most people trust Joe.
4. _____ The speaker and her brother often disagree.
5. _____ The speaker's friend doesn't work hard enough.

6. _____ It might be good that the speaker got a bad grade.

7. _____ Everyone in the family used the same umbrella.

8. _____ The mother and father usually disagree with each other about their children.

9. _____ The new representative can be depended on to do what he promises.

10. _____ The speaker agrees with the president.

Get Down to Business

Improve your ability to use this chapter's idioms in conversation with a couple of your classmates by acting out one or more of the roleplays below.

1. (3 friends)

One of you is moving to another apartment/house. In order to save money, you would rather not hire professional movers to transport your furniture. Instead, you are asking a couple of friends to help you move with a rented truck. Your friends agree, but only if you agree to help them some time in the future too! They think you often ask them for help, but you aren't available often enough when they need help from you.

Use the following idioms in your discussion:

give a hand	**pull together**	**help out**
do a favor	**come through for**	**keep one's word**
give and take	**give a break**	**bend over backwards to**
take turns	**meet one halfway**	**see eye to eye**

2. (employer and employee)

You are looking for an assistant, and one of your current employees is applying. If he/she gets this job, it will be a promotion. In general, you've been very pleased with this employee's performance. However, last month, this employee disagreed with you publicly at a meeting, and now you're worried about hiring him/her for this position because you think you need someone who can support you completely in your work.

Use the following idioms in your interview:

right-hand man or woman	**back up**	**pull together**
give a break	**come through (for)**	**see eye to eye**
help out	**bend over backwards**	

3. (husband, wife, and a friend)

You are about to become parents for the first time, and you have a lot of decisions to make. You are discussing how excited you are about this when your friend asks who is going to be responsible for the child's care: feeding, cleaning, changing diapers, giving care when the baby's sick, etc. Will it be the husband, the wife, or both together? The three of you disagree about what is best for the baby.

Use the following idioms as you discuss this:

meet halfway	**do a favor**	**take turns**
give a hand	**pull together**	**give and take**
see eye to eye	**hand in hand**	**keep one's word**
give a break	**help out**	

4. (1–2 roommates and a possible new roommate)

You've decided that you need another roommate in order to pay your bills. One of your friends has asked to move in, but you know this person is very messy and undependable. However, you've been advertising for a month, and nobody else has applied. You discuss it with your friend, who wants to move in and promises to help.

Use the following idioms in your discussion:

meet one halfway	**take turns**	**bend over backwards to**
give a hand	**pull together**	
keep one's word	**help out**	**give and take**
come through for		

Put It All Together

Reinforce your ability to speak using many of the idioms you've learned so far by acting out one or more of the roleplays below with your classmates.

1. (3–4 parents)

All of you are complaining about how hard it is to find good babysitters and how expensive they are. You've been having a lot of trouble with your babysitters. After complaining for a few minutes, one of you has a brilliant idea: form a "cooperative." You will babysit for each other. It won't cost any money because you will be trading babysitting, and you can be sure that your children will receive good care because you are all friends with each other and know each other well.

Use the following idioms in your discussion:

take turns	**give a hand**	**pull together**
back each other up	**see eye to eye on**	**hand in hand**
give and take	**come through for**	**in the long run**
from now on	**keep track of**	**so far**

2. (3–5 neighbors)

Your neighborhood has been looking dirty lately because there has been so much litter from the area fast-food restaurants. You've decided it's time to organize a campaign against this litter. Tonight, you're having a meeting to discuss how to do this. Because you realize the primary problem is the fast-food restaurants, you are planning to talk to their managers about ways to control the litter.

Use the following idioms as you plan your campaign:

meet one halfway	**give a hand**	**pull together**
back up	**see eye to eye**	**keep one's word**
carry out	**keep track of**	**be about to**
day in and day out	**right away**	**so far**
from now on	**around the clock**	**come through for**

3. (2–3 medical students)

Your big examination was scheduled for next week, but now it's been rescheduled for 2 weeks from now. This is great news because you aren't prepared. All of you have been studying alone until now. Because the exam has been rescheduled, you've decided to spend the next 2 weeks studying together in order to study more efficiently. Each of you plans to study one section of the material in detail, then you'll all get together to go over each other's notes and teach each other.

Use the following idioms as you plan how to study:

take turns	**give a hand**	**pull together**
back up	**hand in hand**	**help out**
come through for	**make good time**	**move back**
put off	**around the clock**	**so far**
	from now on	

4. (a job applicant and an employer)

You are applying for a job as an assistant to a bank manager. You have been working for the bank for 8 years and believe that you know its procedures and the manager well. You know that the manager thinks efficient use of time is extremely important. During your interview, you emphasize how efficient you are and how important you think time is. The manager also expects the assistant to be very responsible, to do work even before being asked to do it, and to work extra hours whenever necessary. You agree with all of this very strongly.

Use the following idioms during the interview:

bend over backwards to	**give a hand**	**pull together**
	keep track of	**bring up to date**

right-hand man or woman √

carry out

on time √

around the clock

day in and day out

ahead of time √

in the long run

Keep the Ball Rolling

Get still more practice with the idioms you've learned so far by participating in a discussion.

Dr. Christine O'Neil was driving home from dinner with friends early one night when she saw someone lying unconscious at the side of the road. She stopped her car, ran to the person, and saw that he'd apparently been hit by a car. She checked his heart and determined that it was beating. She then checked for broken bones and noticed bruises on his head and a broken ankle. She wrapped his head with her scarf to stop the bleeding, then ran to her car telephone to call for an ambulance. She waited with the victim until the ambulance came.

Three weeks later, she got a letter from the victim's lawyer. The victim was suffering from severe headaches and vision problems. He blamed her for improper care and was going to take her to court to sue her for malpractice. Although her insurance will pay the money he asks for if she loses in court, Dr. O'Neill's reputation may suffer from all the publicity.

Imagine that you are Dr. O'Neill's lawyer. What kind of defense will you plan for her? What arguments will you raise as you defend her in court?

Use the following idioms in your defense plans:

do a favor

keep one's word

for good √

back someone up

put off

bend over backwards

help out

right away

for the time being

in the long run

give a hand

come through for

on the spur of the moment

Put a Fine Point on Them

Use the following definitions and examples to help you understand the details of this chapter's idioms when you do the exercises.

1. *meet (one) halfway*—compromise; cooperate by not demanding 100% of what one wants

    If the superpowers would meet each other halfway, we might be able to achieve world peace.
    Mrs. Jackson tried to find a solution to her problem with her neighbor, but her neighbor wouldn't meet her halfway.

2. *take turns*—alternate one after another (+ V + ing)

    Children often have trouble taking turns when they play together with only one toy.
    My husband and I took turns driving to Canada.

3. *bend over backwards to*—(+ V) try very hard to accomplish something

Although I dislike Jane, I bent over backwards to be polite to her.
Politicians bend over backwards to say what people want to hear.

4. *give (someone) a hand*—help

Bill, can you give me a hand with this box?
My roommate never gives a hand with the housework.

5. *pull together* (Int.)—cooperate (requires plural subjects)

During the flood, residents of Smithville had to pull together to survive.
If we pull together, our work will be a lot easier.

6. *right-hand man or woman*—most helpful assistant

The mayor's right-hand man handled the TV reporters' questions.
If I'm your right-hand woman, why don't you give me a higher salary?

7. *back up*—(S) support another's position or opinion

I think the new law is a bad idea, and this newspaper article backs up my opinion.
If you suggest buying a computer to the boss, I'll back you up.

8. *see eye to eye (on something)*—agree

Kathy and I are good friends because we usually see eye to eye.
Max and Andy are always arguing. They don't see eye to eye on anything.

9. *hand in hand*—together

The biology and chemistry departments are working hand in hand on a new genetics project.
Hand in hand, the old woman and her husband solved their financial problems.

10. *keep one's word*—fulfill a promise

Children often find it difficult to keep their word.
Ted said he wouldn't tell my secret, and he kept his word.

11. *help out*—(S) give assistance

Thanks for the loan. You really helped me out.
Can you help my brother out? His car broke down and he needs a lift* to the gas station.

12. *do a favor (for someone)*—(S) do a kindness for someone

You really did Joe a favor when you studied with him. He was afraid of failing the test.
Could you do me a favor? I need help with the party preparations.

13. *give and take*—sharing; cooperation

A good marriage requires give and take between a wife and husband.
World peace will only come through give and take between nations.

14. *give a break*—(S) give a chance

I was an hour late for the test, but the teacher said he'd give me a break. I can take it tomorrow.
Linda didn't have any experience, but the company gave her a break and hired her because they thought she'd learn easily.

---

* A ride.

15. come through (for someone)—satisfy someone's need, often with difficulty

Bill thought he would have to quit school when he couldn't find tuition money, but his parents came through for him.

We needed tickets for the game, but they were sold out.* Finally, Chris came through for us. Now we can all go.

Check It Out

Take a closer look at the conversation from the "Zero In" section if you want to see any words or phrases that you might not have understood.

A New Job

Pat: Excuse me, Mr. LaSalle. Do you have a minute?

LaSalle: Sure Pat, come in. What can I do for you?

Pat: This is a little difficult, so I guess I'll just speak directly. I've been offered another job, and I think I'm going to accept it.

LaSalle: Well, this is a surprise. You've been my **right-hand woman** for almost 5 years. I'll miss you.

Pat: Thank you, Mr. LaSalle. I've really enjoyed working **hand in hand** with you. We've accomplished a lot together.

LaSalle: Yes, we have. You've **given me a hand** with a lot of difficult situations, especially with that Smith contract. I couldn't have succeeded without your help.

Pat: That's not quite true. You and Smith were able to **meet each other halfway**. That's what made the agreement possible.

LaSalle: Yes, well I'll miss your help, nevertheless. Whenever we had problems around here, you always **came through for** us. What kind of offer did you get?

Pat: I've been asked to assist the city's special investigator. It should be a good opportunity for me. But don't worry. I won't forget that you **gave me my first break**. Working with you has been a wonderful opportunity for me.

LaSalle: Are you sure you want to leave? I would **bend over backwards** to keep you here. Isn't there anything I can do to stop you?

Pat: That's very kind of you, but I'm afraid not. I'm very glad to have had the opportunity to work with you.

LaSalle: Well, Pat, if I can ever **do you a favor**, please be sure to call me. I'll be happy to help you.

Pat: Thank you, Mr. LaSalle.

* No more for sale.

A Great Apartment

Joe: You look tired! What've you been doing?

Mike: Looking for an apartment.

Joe: No luck?

Mike: Actually, I found a few, but I want to be sure I find the right place.

Joe: There's an empty apartment in my building.

Mike: Oh yeah? What's it like?

Joe: The usual, I guess. Nothing fancy, but it's in good condition, a good size, and not too expensive.

Mike: Sounds good so far. What about the neighbors?

Joe: They're great.

Mike: Oh yeah?

Joe: Sure. For example, we all **take turns** in the laundry room. Monday is my day to wash clothes.

Mike: So there's only one washer and dryer?

Joe: And we all **pull together** to keep the building in good condition. My next-door neighbor paid for the paint I used to paint our apartments.

Mike: You call that "pulling together"? You did all the work!

Joe: And there's real **give and take** in the building. Everyone helps everyone else. Just last week my neighbors collected enough money to buy a new lawn mower, so it'll be easier for me to cut the grass.

Mike: Sounds to me like you do all the giving and they do all the taking.

Joe: No, no. They're always **helping** me **out**. When I was sick last month, they let me wait an extra week to cut the grass.

Mike: How kind of them!

Joe: What's wrong? You don't seem impressed.

Mike: I guess we don't **see eye to eye** on the definition of good neighbors. You're not lucky to live there!

Joe: Well, talk to Tom. He used to be my roommate. He can **back me up**. He'll tell you how nice it is to live here.

Mike: If it's so nice, why did he leave?

Joe: It was his fault he had to leave.

Mike: He *had* to leave?

Joe: Well he promised to help with the work—like everyone else, but he didn't **keep** his **word**. He just stopped helping.

Mike: Gee, I wonder why!

Finances

4

"Easy come, easy go."

This means that we spend money as fast or as easily as we earn it. In the U.S., this is often true. People aren't in the habit of saving much. Is this true in your country? We can creatively use this expression about areas other than finances. Can you imagine some?

Get Ready

Prepare to hear a conversation by looking at the picture to the left and discussing the questions below with your teacher.

1. What is on the table?
2. Why is it there?
3. What do you think the women are talking about?

Get the Gist

Answer these questions after you listen to the conversation one time.

Laid Off

1. What happened to one woman's job?
2. How worried is she about it? Why?
3. What does her friend think she should do next?
4. What ideas do they have about finding enough money for their plan?

Zero In

Determine the meanings of this chapter's idioms by listening to the conversation again and circling the most likely meaning for each idiom.

1. *laid off*	sleepy	promoted	without a job
2. *in the red*	in debt	angry	doing well
3. *make ends meet*	find a job	stay happy	have enough money
4. *am broke*	am very unhappy	am without money	am sick

5. *did without*	did nothing	managed without things	bought some things
6. *living it up*	living in a big house	saving money	spending money freely
7. *run out of*	have no more	exercise	escape
8. *get out from under*	pay the bills	increase the price	get a new job
9. *make a living*	stay healthy	earn enough money	save money
10. *run*	cost	jog	lose
11. *land on your feet*	solve a problem	jump	fly
12. *be a steal*	be against the law	be surprisingly cheap	be too expensive
13. *break even*	break	depend	earn the amount spent
14. *wear out*	no longer function	take outside	buy cheaply
15. *come up in the world*	fly more often	travel more	become rich and famous

---

Get Your Bearings

Use these exercises to become familiar with the idioms. You may want to refer to the definitions and examples at the end of this chapter while you do them.

Exercise 1: Read each statement then check (√) the statement that means the same thing.

1. When I was a student, I often had to do without things that I'd had when I lived with my parents.

    a. _____ I didn't have enough money to buy a lot of things when I was a student.

    b. _____ Because I was a student, my parents told me not to buy too many things.

2. Joe is actually sorry that he doesn't have to make a living. I don't understand him.

    a. _____ Joe doesn't like to work.

    b. _____ Joe wishes he had to work.

3. It's very strange how easily Joan managed to get out from under. I didn't think she had a job.

    a. _____ I don't know why Joan hasn't been able to pay her bills.

    b. _____ Joan found some money, but I don't know how.

4. We often imagine actors and actresses living it up in Hollywood. But I suspect their lives aren't really so exciting.

   a. _____ We usually think actors and actresses can't live anywhere but Hollywood, but that could be wrong.

   b. _____ We think actors and actresses have a lot of money to spend, but that could be wrong.

5. When inflation is rising quickly, people start having trouble making ends meet.

   a. _____ When there is an inflation problem, people don't like to meet and talk about it.

   b. _____ People just don't have enough money when inflation rises fast.

6. Scott told me the stereo he bought last week was a steal. We have to go talk to him right away.

   a. _____ Scott paid a lot less money for his stereo than he expected to pay. We have to find out where he bought it.

   b. _____ Scott stole his stereo and has offered to steal one for us too. We have to advise him.

7. My husband and I bought a house 5 years ago. If we thought we could break even, we would sell it, but that isn't likely.

   a. _____ We expect to lose money if we sell our house now.

   b. _____ We could make a nice profit if we sold our house soon.

8. Oh Timmy! I don't understand how one little boy can wear out pants so fast.

   a. _____ Timmy wears his pants everywhere.

   b. _____ Timmy gets holes in his pants very quickly.

9. C.O.G. ended the year in the red, so the company president plans to lay off 100 workers in its Chicago office.

   a. _____ One hundred workers will lose their jobs because the C.O.G. president is very angry.

   b. _____ Because C.O.G. is losing money, 100 workers will lose their jobs.

10. All of my high school classmates got together for our 10-year reunion party. Everyone was surprised how Tom Kennedy had come up in the world.

    a. _____ Tom was not very popular and had little money when he was a high school student.

    b. _____ Tom is not very popular or wealthy now.

11. I've been broke so long. Now I can live it up.

    a. _____ I have a little more money now.

    b. _____ I've been sick for a while and need some fun now.

12. I ran out of thread while I was making curtains for the livingroom.

    a. _____ I left the livingroom while I was making the curtains.

    b. _____ I need to buy thread.

13. We expected the police to take the old man's furniture and put him out on the street. Of course, he landed on his feet.

    a. _____ The old man was thrown out of his apartment.

    b. _____ The old man is living in his apartment with his furniture.

14. What does a young, healthy dog or puppy run?

    a. _____ We are asking about the dog's cost.

    b. _____ We are asking about the dog's physical health.

Exercise 2: Circle the letter of the *best* idiom to complete the sentences.

1. I'm not sure how I'll _____. Maybe I'll be a psychologist or a teacher.

    a. live it up
    b. land on my feet
    c. make a living

2. Companies that are _____ often go bankrupt.

    a. in the red
    b. in the black
    c. a steal

3. After the manufacturing companies left the area and the workers were laid off, many of the other businesses _____ too.

    a. made ends meet
    b. went broke
    c. broke even

4. Many young children whose families have no home to live in _____ the things they need.

    a. wear out
    b. do without
    c. live it up

5. It can be very hard for single parents to _____. There never seems to be enough money for everything the family needs.

    a. come up in the world
    b. make ends meet
    c. wear out

6. After Tom lost his job and his wife, we expected him to go crazy. But he
_____. He now has a better job and is planning to get married soon.

   a. lived it up
   b. landed on his feet
   c. ran out

7. My new TV had a 2-year guarantee, but the electonic circuitry _____ in just 14 months. I'll have to return it.

   a. ran out
   b. went broke
   c. wore out

8. Kathy is celebrating her promotion. She's invited all of us to go out tonight and _____, her treat.*

   a. run
   b. live it up
   c. get out from under

9. I've been sick so long, that I'm _____. I spent all my money on doctors and hospitals.

   a. breaking even
   b. running out
   c. broke

10. Most people try to be careful with their money so that they will always be
_____.

   a. in the black
   b. in the red
   c. a steal

11. Maggie had been a homemaker for most of her adult life. When her husband died, she had no idea how to _____.

   a. run out
   b. make ends meet
   c. break even

12. A good VCR used to _____ about $1500, but now you can find one much more cheaply.

   a. be a steal
   b. do without
   c. run

Exercise 3: Ken, a full-time college student, lives in an apartment off his college campus. Even though he has a part-time job, he's been having money problems

* She'll pay for it.

recently. Below are letters between Ken and his parents about his financial problems. Fill in the blanks with appropriate idioms from the list below.

was a steal	**laid off**	**in the red**
live it up	**am broke**	**ran out of**
get out from under	**do without**	**land on your own feet**
making ends meet	**break even**	**came up in the world**
	wearing out	

Dear Mom and Dad,

Hi! How's it going? Playing a lot of tennis lately?

School's going fine. Just got back a test and I aced* it (naturally!). Seriously, my classes are hard, but I'm managing to do OK so far.

Unfortunately, I have a bit of a problem. I'm having some trouble _____

_____ .

My rent was due last week, but I _____. I don't have any money left in my bank account. And I have to make my car payment at the end of

next week. Would you mind helping me _____? If you could just lend me a few hundred dollars, I promise I'll pay you back soon.

Love,
Ken

Dear Kenneth,

We were very happy to hear that you are doing well in school. No, we haven't had much time to play tennis recently because both of us have been very busy at work recently.

Kenneth, we're becoming worried about your ability to manage money. We understand that college students like to _____ with parties, movies, fancy cars, and lots of pizza, but you also have to learn how to _____

_____ some things. Your problem is that you have a "champagne appetite on a beer budget."**

All our Love,
Mom and Dad

Dear Mom and Dad,

Just got your letter. I was pretty disappointed at first. But I think I understand

now. You guys have plenty of money—you just forget what it's like to be _____

_____ .

---

* Got the highest grade (A) easily.
** Want elegant possessions without enough money to pay for them.

Yesterday, my car _____ gas, and I didn't have money to buy more. Well, maybe I should sell my car. But I don't think I'll be able

to _____ on it. Are you sure you can't lend me some money?

Ken

Dear Son,

Your attitude about money continues to disappoint us. We think it's important

for you to learn how to _____, without our help. If we help you every time you have financial problems now, what will you do when you no longer have us?

And by the way, you are wrong about us. Your mother and I were not always

wealthy. We _____ only because of hard work. When you were

just a year old, I was _____ from my job for almost 6 months.

That was a hard time for us. I remember seeing your clothes _____, and I felt terrible because I didn't have enough money to replace them.

If you need money now, you should sell both your car and your stereo. And in the future, you shouldn't spend more than you earn.

Mom and Dad

Mom and Dad,

Well, I did what you suggested and sold my car. The guy that bought it thought

it _____. He was really happy with the price, and I got enough money to pay my bills. But there's no way that I'm going to sell my stereo! I need it to help me study.

Love,
Ken

Tune In

Improve your ability to hear and understand idioms by listening to several statements and answering the questions below T for True or F for False.

_____ *1.* The woman is going to return the boots tomorrow because they were too expensive.

_____ *2.* The woman thinks it might sell for less than $90.

_____ *3.* The woman thinks music will lead to a good career.

_____ *4.* William has a problem.

_____ *5.* Now is probably the best time to buy a VCR.

_____ *6.* The man did badly on the examination.

_____ *7.* In the long run, the television wasn't a bargain.

_____ *8.* The child has as many toys as the father did when he was a child.

_____ *9.* Both the man and the woman have no money.

_____ *10.* The woman doesn't have enough money to pay the rent.

Get Down to Business

Improve your ability to use this chapter's idioms in conversation with a couple of your classmates by acting out one or more of the roleplays below.

1. (2 friends)

First friend: You have been spending too much money lately and you've just lost your job. Now you have to make a car payment and a mortgage (house) payment or you'll lose your car and a $2.5 million house. Unfortunately, your bank account is empty. You know your best friend probably has some extra money, so you ask him or her for a loan. You think he or she will agree because of your friendship.

Second friend: You care a lot about your friend and would like to help your friend out. You're not worried much about losing your money. But your friend has always been irresponsible about money and has always had inflated ideas about his or her future. This seems to be a good time for your friend to learn some responsibility. You'd prefer, therefore, not to lend the money and hope your friend learns a lesson from having to sell his or her possessions and deal with his or her debts.

Use the following idioms:

laid off	**in the red**	**make ends meet**
be broke	**live it up**	**make a living**
land on one's feet	**get out from under**	**come up in the world**
do without	**run**	**break even**

2. (4 classmates)

Twenty years after you've graduated, your school is holding a reunion, a party that all the old classmates attend in order to share news about their lives.

Classmate #1: Everyone has always expected you to do well in business because you were always creative and always loved money. At one time, you were doing very well, but lately you've fallen on hard times (you're not doing well anymore). You've lost your job. This is embarrassing for you and you'd prefer to talk about your achievements of a few years ago.

Classmate #2: You also were expected to do very well, but you chose not to. You believe that money corrupts people, and you have spent your life trying to live simply, without struggling for money or power. Of course, your former classmates find this hard to believe.

Classmate #3: Nobody ever expected you to "amount to" much. (You were thought to be a "zero"!) Now you come to the reunion in a limousine with a fancy suit and beautiful clothes and jewelry. You've made it! (You're successful.)

Classmate #4: You are a single parent with two children in elementary school. Your job doesn't pay well so it's pretty hard for you to work and take care of your children too. But your family is fairly happy, even considering your children often need things that they can't have because there isn't enough money.

Use the following idioms:

laid off	**in the red**	**make ends meet**
be broke	**do without**	**live it up**
run out of	**make a living**	**run**
wear out	**get out from under**	**come up in the world**
	land on one's feet	

3. (a brother and sister)

In the United States, and perhaps in your country, it is possible for people to borrow money from a bank even if they cannot guarantee that they will be able to pay it back. They do this by finding a friend or family member to "co-sign the loan," that is, to sign the loan contract and promise to pay the money back if the loan recipient is unable to do so.

Brother: You have a great idea to buy a little shop near your house and go into business, but you need to borrow $30,000 to "get it off the ground." (get it started) You have almost no money in the bank and you don't own your house. You do own a 3-year-old car and you have a pretty good job. You've decided to ask your sister to co-sign the loan for you.

Sister: You love your brother very much and you believe in him. However, he has no business experience, and you're very worried that, if the business fails, you'll have to use all of your savings to pay off the loan. After discussing it with your brother, you agree to do it, convinced that he will be successful.

Use the following idioms in your conversation:

in the red	**make ends meet**	**go/be broke**
do without	**live it up**	**break even**
make a living	**run**	**land on one's feet**
be a steal	**come up in the world**	**get out from under**

4. (brother and sister or 2 friends)

You lent your friend money to start a business, but it is clear that the business is failing and there's no money to pay off (complete payments for) the loan.

Brother: You're sorry, but you're going to have to default (not pay) on the loan. You promise your sister to pay her back sometime in the future.

Sister: You are really angry. You'll have to continue paying this loan for 5 more years. You won't have any money for clothes, entertainment, "extras," and you won't even be able to think about getting married until the loan is paid off. You can't believe your brother used all $30,000 in only 6 months.

Use these idioms:

in the red	**make ends meet**	**go/be broke**
do without	**live it up**	**break even**
make a living	**run**	**land on one's feet**
	get out from under	

Put It All Together

Reinforce your ability to speak using many of the idioms you've learned so far by acting out one or more of the roleplays below with your classmates.

1. (wife and husband)

You and your husband have been looking at houses to buy for several months, and it seems you've finally found your dream house. It has all the characteristics you've been hoping for. But there's one problem: it's more expensive than you were planning on. This house would be a very good investment, but you must decide whether to spend more on the house than you had planned. You disagree about this.

Use the following idioms:

in the long run	**every so often**	**put off**
on the spur of the moment	**bend over backwards to**	**live it up**
		in the red
make ends meet	**up to date**	**meet someone halfway**
run	**get out from under**	**from now on**

2. (a student and parents)

You've been planning to go to college for a long time. You've had a job after school and during summer vacations for years. But now you have only 3 months until college starts and you don't have enough money for the first year. Your parents really want you to get a college education, but they have only enough money to live on. You are discussing the possibility that your parents can help you find a way to get the money.

Use the following idioms in your discussion:

make ends meet	**run out of**	**do without**
break even	**pull together**	**help out**
come through for	**put off**	**call off**
look forward to	**carry out**	**just around the corner**
so far	**land on one's feet**	**fall through**

3. (a car owner and a possible buyer)

You want to sell your car because you need cash fast. Your car is only 2 years old, and you haven't driven it very much. You are asking $8,000 for it. It originally cost you $13,000 and you still owe $6,000 on the bank loan that helped you to buy it. You think it's a wonderful deal at $8,000. The possible buyer is looking for a better deal on a car. He/she doesn't want to pay more than $5,000.

Use the following idioms as you discuss the sale of the car:

make ends meet	**(not) break even**	**run (cost)**
get out from under	**help out**	**do a favor**
(not) see eye to eye	**give a break**	**so far**
be a steal		**meet one halfway**

4. (an employee and the manager)

You have been working at this company for more than 1 year and haven't had a raise yet (an increase in your salary). You believe you have shown that you are a very responsible employee and you deserve more money. You've decided to ask your manager for a raise. The manager says the company wasn't doing very well 2 years ago. Although it's doing better now, the manager doesn't want to give raises until the finances of the company are assured.

Use the following idioms in your conversation:

make ends meet	**in the red**	**go broke**
come up in the world	**help out**	**so far**
do a favor	**give a break**	**come through for**
give a hand	**put off**	**keep track of**

Keep the Ball Rolling

Get still more practice with the idioms you've learned so far by participating in a discussion.

In the U.S. and in other countries, a special financial program exists to prevent people from becoming completely destitute. It is called public assistance. In this program, people receive a rather small amount of money each month to pay for housing, food, and clothing. Sometimes, they receive coupons that can be redeemed for food.

Imagine that you are a Public Assistance Caseworker. Read each of the following situations and decide whether the person should receive public assistance or not. Because you will be making recommendations to your boss, you must prepare your reasons for each decision carefully. What should be done when you recommend no public assistance?

Use the idioms below in your discussion and recommendations:

laid off	**make ends meet**	**be broke**
do without	**live it up**	**make a living**
break even	**come up in the world**	**give and take**
in the long run	**for the time being**	**for good**
about to	**put off**	**look forward to**
land on one's feet	**help someone out**	**give a hand**
give someone a break		

A. Julianne Reynolds, 22 years old

Single mother
3 children, all under 5 years old
High school diploma
Has never had a job
Husband disappeared
Is healthy

B. Stanley and June Robinson

58 and 54 years old
An adult daughter and adult son
4 teenaged grandchildren
Stanley, a retired factory worker
June, never worked outside the home
Invested their savings in the stock market and lost most of it
Stanley is fairly healthy; June's health is failing a little.

C. Roger Haley, 31 years old

Never married
High school diploma
Has had several short-term jobs
Was arrested for one small theft but was never convicted
Wants to study carpentry in technical school
Is healthy

D Ed and Tanya Taylor

Both 26 years old
2 children, ages 4 and 6
Ed, high school graduate, jobless construction worker
Tanya, 1 year of college, used to be a secretary.
Both healthy

Put a Fine Point on Them

Use the following definitions and examples to help you understand the details of this chapter's idioms when you do the exercises.

1. make ends meet—have enough money for expenses

When inflation is high, it's hard to make ends meet.
Newlyweds often have trouble making ends meet.

2. run out of (something)—have no more in supply

I always run out of money before the end of the month.
We ran out of gas before we got to the ocean, so we had to walk to a gas station.

3. *wear out*—no longer function

> It's expensive to buy clothes for children because the clothes wear out so fast.
>
> The dial on our TV wore out. We have to replace it before we can watch the TV again.

4. *be a steal*—be a very good bargain; be surprisingly cheap

> These shoes are a steal. You won't find a better price.
>
> Two for the price of one? That's a steal.

5. *do without*—manage without something in order to save money or because there isn't enough money for it

> I can do without new shoes, but I can't do without food.
>
> Very poor people do without many necessities.

6. *get out from under*—recover from financial problems; pay all of one's bills

> After so many hospital bills, it was hard for the Kress family to get out from under.
>
> Getting out from under after losing all your money takes years.

7. *land on one's feet*—get out of trouble, often with an advantage

> It looked like Sam would lose his job, but he landed on his feet. He has a better job now.
>
> Donna owes 3 months' rent, but she always lands on her feet. She'll probably win a lot of money or something.

8. *lay off*—(S)temporarily dismiss someone from a job

> The corporation laid 1,000 employees off when it lost a government contract.
>
> When the biggest company here relocated to Los Angeles, both Jim and his wife were laid off.

9. *live it up*—spend money freely

> Let's live it up Saturday. We'll have dinner at the best restaurant and go to the theater.
>
> After exams were over, the students lived it up at all of the discos downtown.

10. *make a living*—earn enough money to pay one's living expenses (+ Verb + ing)

> I'd like to make a living by shopping. It's my biggest talent.
>
> Victor is the only person I know who earns a living by selling poems.

11. *run*—cost

> Luxury cars run a lot of money.
>
> Old houses run less money than new ones, but they often need more repairs.

12. *in the red*—in debt (compare with *in the black*, not in debt)

> I finished the month in the red.
>
> When a company is in the red, people get laid off.
>
> The company is now in the black because of increased demand for its product.

13. *be/go broke*—have no money

> Can you lend me a few bucks*? I'm broke.
> Frank is usually broke by the end of the month.
> Everybody was surprised that Joe went broke because he was always so careful with his money.

14. *come up in the world*—gain wealth, success, importance

> Wow! You have new clothes and a new apartment. You're coming up in the world.
> With her graduation just around the corner, Tanya will be coming up in the world.

15. *break even (on something)*—sell for the amount of money invested

> The Wilsons were expecting to make a profit when they sold their house, but they only broke even.
> Dale was hoping just to break even on the sale of her car, but she actually made a little extra money.

Check It Out

Take a closer look at the conversation from the "Zero In" section if you want to see any words or phrases that you might not have understood.

Laid Off

Ann: Terry, what's wrong?

Terry: I got **laid off** from my job.

Ann: Oh no. Why?

Terry: The company has decided to decrease production. That means they need fewer workers for the time being.

Ann: I'm so sorry. You must feel awful. Maybe you'll get your job back soon.

Terry: No. Probably not. Actually, I'm not very surprised. I've known for some time that the company was **in the red**. It started losing money 3 years ago.

Ann: What will you do? How will you **make ends meet**? Would you like to borrow some money from me?

Terry: Thanks, but **I'm** not **broke**. I've been saving money for emergencies. I guess this is an emergency.

Ann: How did you manage to save money? Didn't you say your job didn't pay a lot?

Terry: Yes, but I **did without** a few things—like fewer movies, fewer dinners in restaurants. In other words, I stopped **living it up** after I realized the company was in trouble. I just stopped spending so much money.

Ann: That was smart. But what will you do after you **run out of** the money you saved?

---

* Dollars.

Terry: I'll have to get another job. Don't worry. I'll find a way to **get out from under**. I won't have to live on the street.

Ann: Maybe you can **make a living** by selling your breads and cakes. Everyone says they love them.

Terry: That's a great idea. I wonder how much money it would **run** to start my own business? Do you think it would cost a lot?

Ann: I don't know. But I'm sure you're not going to let this job layoff destroy your life. You're going to **land on your feet**.

Terry: Absolutely. But I have to find a way to get enough money to start a business.

Ann: I guess you could sell your car. It's worth about $10,000, isn't it? If someone bought it for about $7,500, it would **be a steal**. Who wouldn't want a bargain like that?

Terry: Yeah, but there's a problem. I couldn't **break even** if I sold my car. I still owe the bank a lot of money for it.

Ann: Oh. Well, anyway, you would need your car to deliver all the breads and cakes.

Terry: Good point! I wouldn't want to **wear out** a new pair of shoes every month. Shoes are almost as expensive as cars!

Ann: You're crazy! Listen, I think you need some help. Why don't we go into business together? You can be the creative genius, and I'll take care of the business end. I have enough money saved to help to start the business.

Terry: Really? What a great idea. Then we can **come up in the world** together.

Ann: Of course! We're gonna be rich!

Authority

5

"The buck stops here."

This statement originated with former U.S. President Harry Truman. It is commonly used now to mean "I have the ultimate authority." We also use a popular phrase "pass the buck," which means "claim that someone else has the authority; don't take responsibility." In your country, would people be more likely to "pass the buck" or to say "The buck stops here"? In what types of situations could you use these?

Get Ready

Prepare to hear a conversation by looking at the picture to the left and discussing the questions below with your teacher.

1. What does the man seem to be doing?
2. What does the police officer seem to doing?
3. Why do you think the officer is spending time with the man?

Get the Gist

Answer these questions after you listen to the conversation one time.

The Bad Driver

1. Why did the police officer decide to stop the driver?
2. What was the driver's attitude toward the police officer at first?
3. Why wasn't the driver worried in the beginning about being stopped?
4. What did the police officer think about Judge Horton?

Zero In

Determine the meanings of this chapter's idioms by listening to the conversation again and circling the most likely meaning for each idiom.

1. *going by the book*	obeying the rules	reading a book	giving little books
2. *according to*	because of	in the opinion of	instead of
3. *talk back*	answer without respect	discuss deeply	ask questions
4. *calls for*	shouts	requests	requires

5. *who's who*	people's problems	people's identities	troublemakers
6. *pull strings*	cause trouble	collect for future use	get help from someone important
7. *put an end to*	put in jail	make a law against	stop
8. *call the shots*	use a gun	give orders	obey
9. *toe the line*	behave correctly	walk straight	wait
10. *go through proper channels*	call on the radio	follow established procedures	wait for instructions
11. *red tape*	colorful decoration	loss of freedom	complex procedures
12. *take that up with*	remove from	give to	discuss with
13. *throw the book at*	punish strongly	make you study	be smarter
14. *crack down on*	break	become angry	be strict with
15. *get out of line*	cause trouble	forget	wait too long

Get Your Bearings

Use these exercises to become familiar with the idioms. You may want to refer to the definitions and examples at the end of this chapter while you do them.

Exercise 1: Mark each sentence T for true or F for false.

_____ 1. Parents should encourage their children to talk back to their teachers as often as they can.

_____ 2. People would vote for a leader who promised to put an end to war.

_____ 3. People who enjoy calling the shots would be happy working on assembly lines in factories.

_____ 4. Soldiers in the army must be prohibited from toeing the line.

_____ 5. Red tape is useful during a New Year celebration.

_____ 6. Police in many countries are trying to crack down on drug sales.

_____ 7. It's not a good idea to get out of line when visiting a foreign country.

_____ 8. People who are included in a book called *Who's Who* are probably very influential people.

_____ 9. A person who doesn't know many people will probably be able to pull strings easily.

_____ 10. People with influential friends don't always have to go through proper channels.

_____ *11.* Artistic people are likely to go by the book when they are creating new works.

_____ *12.* Parents who often throw the book at their children are not strict enough with their children.

_____ *13.* We might be happy if government leaders call for lower taxes.

_____ *14.* Some diseases can be alleviated by thinking happy thoughts, according to some health professionals.

_____ *15.* When we think there is too much homework, we might take it up with the teacher.

Exercise 2: Choose the phrase that best completes the following sentences.

1. For _____ to do their jobs well, they ought to go by the book.

    a. police
    b. artists
    c. newspaper reporters

2. On television, I saw a large group of citizens calling for _____.

    a. fewer jobs
    b. the mayor's resignation
    c. an increase in bus fares

3. Jane wanted to make a change in her job description. Her friends urged her to take it up with _____.

    a. her mother
    b. her other friends
    c. her boss

4. If you want to _____, you have to go through proper channels.

    a. lose weight
    b. go to college
    c. get a haircut

5. We weren't surprised when _____ started calling the shots, even though it had been our project from the beginning.

    a. the new employee
    b. the teenager
    c. the department head

6. _____ threw the book at me after I came back from my mysterious trip late at night and very dirty.

    a. My parents
    b. My co-workers
    c. The grocery clerk

7. The candidate promised that she would crack down on _____.

   a. sunbathing at the beach
   b. parking in public parking lots
   c. selling cigarettes to children

8. Children who get out of line at school _____.

   a. get good grades
   b. get punished
   c. learn a lot

9. The director told _____ if they didn't toe the line, they would not be permitted to return to the institute.

   a. the parents
   b. the students
   c. her grandparents

10. The earth may continue to become warmer and warmer in the long run, according to _____.

    a. a recent news article
    b. me
    c. my little sister

11. Because _____ talked back, he was not permitted to join the rest of the group for lunch.

    a. the lawyer
    b. the three-year-old
    c. my co-worker

12. It's incredible how much red tape there is when you _____.

    a. borrow a library book
    b. get married
    c. go grocery shopping

13. I think it's about time we put an end to _____.

    a. high schools
    b. driver's licenses
    c. smoking in public

14. I know Murphy will be able to pull strings for us because he _____.

    a. is strong
    b. knows some important people
    c. is intelligent

15. He thinks he should be in the newest edition of the book *Who's Who* because he's so _____.

    a. important
    b. intelligent
    c. funny

Exercise 3: You are a well-respected lawyer in your country. People travel long distances just to get your advice. Read the summaries of their problems below and write a sentence giving advice, using the idioms in the list.

pull strings	**throw the book at him**	**go through proper channels**
crack down on them	**toe the line**	**call for**
who's who	**red tape**	**talk back**
take it up with	**call the shots**	

1. My son applied to the best university in our country. His grades were very good in high school, and his teachers wrote good recommendation letters for him, but he wasn't accepted by the school. I asked the director, a good friend of mine, why not. He said there were many qualified applicants, but the school could only accept a limited number. We really want him in that school. What should we do?

_____

2. Our police department has a good reputation for maintaining order in the city. Last week, one of our officers chased a car that was driving too fast on a residential street. The driver almost hit a group of children playing near the street. When the officer finally caught the car, he discovered the driver was the mayor's son, who had drunk a little alcohol. What should we do? _____

_____

3. My aunt and her family want to immigrate to your country very much. Unfortunately, they haven't been able to get official permission for this. It would be very easy for them to enter your country without permission, and they have plenty of money. What do you recommend? _____

4. My apartment is terrible. Sometimes the heat doesn't work, very often the water doesn't work, and there are holes in one wall. I'd like the problems to be repaired. Who should I talk to first? _____

5. I hate my college. It's one of the most prestigious schools in my country, but it's much too strict. Last week, they threatened to expel me because I argued with a teacher about a grade she gave me. I'll be graduating at the end of this year, and I know my future will be assured with a degree from this college, but I can't tolerate this situation until then. I want to have fun. What should I do? _____

_____

6. We just had an election in our neighborhood for the Community Council. According to the "official" results, a certain man won. But I happen to know that the election results were "fixed." The election wasn't honest. There are a few people who know about this. What should we do? _____

7. Some teenagers in our neighborhood stay out late at night, make a lot of noise, and sometimes threaten people. We're becoming afraid to go out of our homes at night. We've called the police, and they chase the kids away, but the kids always come back later. What should we do? _____

8. My wife and I want to borrow money from the bank to start our own business. Because the loan is insured by the government, there are dozens of forms and applications to fill out. Isn't there a simpler way? We don't want to handle all of that paperwork if we can avoid it. _____

9. I was made manager of my department 2 months ago. All of my co-workers were really happy for me, but I have a problem. My co-workers are also my friends. Since I've been made manager, they won't listen to me. If I don't find a way to get them to pay serious attention to my directions, I'll lose my job. What can I do? _____

10. I'm new in town, and I need a job. I'm a newspaper reporter with 5 years' experience. I applied at the *Gazette*, but they said they don't hire people that they don't know. I don't know anyone at the *Gazette*. What can I do? _____
_____

Tune In

Improve your ability to hear and understand idioms by listening to several news reports and answering the questions below T for True or F for False.

A. (prison trouble)

_____ *1.* The prisoners have ended their rebellion.

_____ *2.* The prisoners will have a meeting with the director.

_____ *3.* The prison director will not consider the prisoners' demands.

_____ *4.* The prison director has promised not to punish the prisoners for their rebellion.

B. (election news)

_____ *5.* Joe Berkowitz is his wife's boss at work.

_____ *6.* Berkowitz's wife may not be qualified for her job.

_____ *7.* Berkowitz admits giving his wife a little help to get the job.

_____ *8.* A believable source says that Mrs. Berkowitz got the job without unfair help.

C. (more election news)

_____ *9.* These candidates believe there isn't enough effort now to control crime in the city.

_____ *10.* The first candidate wants to force business people to hire more guards.

_____ *11.* The second candidate wants to make it easier to put criminals in jail and to give them stricter punishments.

_____ *12.* The second candidate believes that the first candidate is only interested in important people.

Get Down to Business

Improve your ability to use this chapter's idioms in conversation with a couple of your classmates by acting out one or more of the roleplays below.

1. (3 friends)

You are discussing whether or not you should join the army. One of you believes eventually you'll all be drafted (required to join). It's better to join now than have one's life interrupted at a bad time. Besides, the army teaches a boy how to be a man (or a girl how to be a woman) and gives good job experience.

The second friend would rather go to college first and then join the army as an officer who gives orders rather than takes them. He/she also thinks it's possible to avoid going into the army if one knows the right people.

The third hopes never to go into the army and is trying to convince the others not to join either. He/she says life should be fun, and army life is miserable. Soldiers can never do the things they want to do. Their lives are not their own anymore.

Use the following idioms in your conversation:

go by the book	**according to**	**pull strings**
talk back	**put an end to**	**call the shots**
toe the line	**red tape**	**take up with**
throw the book at	**crack down on**	**get out of line**
	go through channels	

2. (3 classmates)

You are very unhappy with your course in ＿＿＿ (you choose). You believe the teacher gives too much homework, doesn't explain things well enough, doesn't give enough time for students to ask questions, and doesn't allow students to be creative on homework or tests. The teacher, in short, is too authoritarian. You are discussing these problems and what you might do to correct them. You are considering withdrawing from the class, but it's very difficult to get permission to do this.

NOTE: In the U.S., when students are having a problem with a course or a teacher, they usually talk to the teacher directly about it. It is considered impolite to talk to the director or principal without first having talked to the teacher.

Use the following idioms in your discussion:

go by the book	**according to**	**pull strings**
talk back	**call for**	**put an end to**
call the shots	**toe the line**	**go through channels**
take up with	**throw the book at**	**crack down on**
	get out of line	

3. (2–3 friends out shopping together, a security guard)

You've been having a wonderful time looking at all of the merchandise in the stores and buying some of it too. You've been laughing and joking. Without realizing it, one of you left a store carrying something you didn't pay for and now a security guard wants to arrest you for shoplifting. The guard is going to call the police. All of you are trying to convince the guard that you did not intend to steal store merchandise. One of you knows the owner of the store. You had dinner together at a mutual friend's home last week. This is the guard's first day on the job. The guard has been told by the boss that shoplifting has been an epidemic in the store.

Use the following idioms in your discussion:

go by the book	**according to**	**talk back**
call for	**who's who**	**put an end to**
toe the line	**take up with**	**red tape**
throw the book at	**crack down on**	**get out of line**

4. (a customs agent and one or two travelers)

You've just come back from a wonderful trip to _____ (you decide). While you were there, you bought some _____ (you decide). You are now in the airport in your city, talking to the custom's agent. You are trying to keep your purchase a secret so that you won't have to pay duty (a tax) on your purchase. The agent is suspicious of you and searches your luggage.

Use the following idioms in your conversation:

throw the book at	**according to**	**put an end to**
get out of line	**talk back**	**take up with**
red tape	**pull strings**	**crack down on**
go by the book	**call the shots**	

Put It All Together

Reinforce your ability to speak using many of the idioms you've learned so far by acting out one or more of the roleplays below with your classmates.

1. (a car owner and a friend)

According to the law in your area, your car must be inspected twice a year. It's now time for an inspection, but you're pretty sure your car won't pass because of a problem with the carburetor (the part of the car where gasoline becomes energy). It is a very expensive problem to fix, but you really need your car for your job. A friend of yours knows a mechanic who will give you the inspection approval sticker for a certain amount of money. This is clearly illegal, and you're very nervous about doing this. You need the inspection approval before the end of the week.

Use the following idioms as you discuss this with your friend:

in time	**for the time being**	**do a favor**
wear out	**throw the book at**	**red tape**
go by the book	**pull strings**	**help out**
do without	**call for**	**carry out**

2. (a school director, an assistant, and one or both parents)

You want your 5-year-old child to have every advantage in his life. Therefore, you've decided that he should attend the Middlemount School for the Socially Advantaged. You are now having a meeting with the school's director, who informs you that your child is not qualified to go to Middlemount because all Middlemount children must enroll at the school by the time they are 4 years old. You are 1 year late. You must convince the director to make an exception in your case.

Use the following idioms in your discussion:

on time	**move back**	**fall through**
look forward to	**give a break**	**meet one halfway**
do a favor	**come up in the world**	**do without**
pull strings	**take up with**	**go by the book**
go through channels	**who's who**	**red tape**
in the long run		

3. (a driver, a friend, and 1 or 2 government employees)

The city says that you have received so many parking tickets that the city government has put a "boot" on your car—a metal device on your rear wheel that prohibits movement of your car. They won't remove it until you pay for parking tickets—which total more than $400. But it's not your fault; you've never even had a parking ticket. However, they refuse to believe you. They suggest that you find someone with more power in city government and ask for help or just pay the fines. But you're new in this city, and you don't have $400.

Use the following idioms in your conversation:

throw the book at	**who's who**	**put an end to**
pull strings	**red tape**	**crack down on**
keep track of	**around the clock**	**see eye to eye**
be broke	**do without**	**bend over backwards to**
give a break	**so far**	

4. (an animal lover and 1 or 2 police officers)

You have loved animals (dogs? cats? You choose.) for many years. Every time a stray animal comes to your door, you take it in. As a result, you now have almost 30 animals living in your house. After asking you to get rid of some of them, your neighbors have finally called the police. In your city, it is against the law to have so many animals living in one residential unit. The police say you must remove 27 of the animals from your home, but how can you choose? You love them all. Instead, you try to convince the city police to let you keep them by pointing out how well cared for they are.

Use the following idioms in your discussion:

go through channels	**according to**	**put an end to**
take up with	**go by the book**	**crack down on**
meet one halfway	**keep one's word**	**help out**
for good	**do without**	**call for**

Keep the Ball Rolling

Get still more practice with the idioms you've learned so far by participating in a discussion.

Euthanasia, also known as mercy killing, has been a controversial topic for many years. Nowadays, a new variation on mercy killing involves people who feel that they cannot live a fulfilling, painfree life asking their doctors to help them die. In some countries this is legal. Read the following case studies and imagine that you are each patient's doctor. Would you agree to assist the patient with his suicide? Why or why not? Use the idioms below when you explain your decision.

1. Roger Murphy, 52, has been suffering from liver cancer for the past 2 months. Each day, he takes pain-killing drugs, but they no longer work very well, and he feels horrible pain all day and all night. He often has to go to the hospital, and his hospital and doctors' bills have amounted to many thousands of dollars so far. Roger has been paying for all of this from his savings, money he had hoped to leave to his children after he died. The doctors have told Roger that there is no hope for his cancer to be cured; it was discovered too late. After discussing the problem with his family, and getting their approval, he has decided to ask his doctor to give him a drug that will allow him to die in his sleep.

2. Janet Morrison, 29, was in a skiing accident 5 months ago and was left paralyzed from the neck down. She is able to talk and eat, but she cannot move her arms, hands, legs, or feet. She must spend all of her days and nights in bed, cared for by family members or friends. Janet was always a very independent, active person. She is extremely unhappy in her present condition. She is overwhelmed by the possibility of spending the next 40 or 50 years in bed, depending on other people and not living a life of her own. She wants to say a happy goodbye to family and friends, then die.

Use the following idioms when you explain your decisions:

go by the book	**keep one's word**	**go broke**
wear out	**make ends meet**	**help out**
red tape	**go through channels**	**give a hand**
call for	**put an end to**	**run**
in the long run	**for good**	**right away**
in time	**call off**	**put off**
on the spur of the moment	**carry out**	**bend over backwards to**
	back up	

Put a Fine Point on Them

Use the following definitions and examples to help you understand the details of this chapter's idioms when you do the exercises.

1. *go through (proper) channels*—follow the bureaucratic, formal procedures

   To get a visa, I had to go through channels.
   Sometimes people don't have to go through proper channels if they know influential people.

2. *throw the book at*—give the strongest punishment; talk to very strongly

   I threw the book at my son after he got home 3 hours late.
   The judge threw the book at the defendant, who was convicted of murder. The murderer was sentenced to life in prison.

3. *who's who*—who the important people are; everyone's identity

   We can accomplish a lot if we know who's who in the government.
   It's important to find out who's who when you start a new job.

4. *according to someone or something*—in the opinion of an expert or knowledgeable source

   According to seismologists, we can expect an earthquake soon.
   Children learn in several stages, according to Piaget.

5. *get out of line*—disobey, cause trouble, misbehave

   Students who get out of line are sometimes expelled from school.
   If you get out of line too often on this job, you'll be fired.

6. *put an end to something*—cause something to stop

   The government would like to put an end to cigarette smoking in public.
   Our boss put an end to extra-long lunch hours.

7. *take up (something with someone)*—(S) discuss a problem with someone who has the power to solve it

   I need a raise. I'm going to take it up with my boss.
   The librarian will have to take up funding for new books with the director.

8. *talk back (to someone)*—answer disrespectfully

   Polite children don't talk back to their parents.
   It's wise not to talk back to police officers.

9. *red tape*—complex bureaucratic procedures or paperwork (often used with the verb phrase "cut through," meaning to avoid or do quickly)

   Getting a driver's license involves some red tape.
   People often have to cut through a lot of red tape to immigrate to another country.

10. *toe the line*—obey; do one's duties; behave correctly

    Soldiers have to toe the line.
    You'd better toe the line in high school if you want to go to college.

11. *pull strings*—achieve a goal through unusual help from an important person.

    They told us the hotel had no more rooms for the night, but Bill pulled a few strings, and now we have a great room. He knew the manager.
    The airline says all the seats on its Saturday flight are booked, but I think I can pull some strings. We'll get our seats.

12. *call for*—require, demand

> The ruling party called for new elections.
> The police are calling for longer sentences* for convicted criminals.

13. *crack down on (someone)*—become very strict with

> Jenny's parents are cracking down on her because her grades weren't good enough.
> The government is cracking down on drug sellers.

14. *go by the book*—do something according to the rules; not be creative or flexible

> When applying for a visa, it's best to go by the book.
> Sam usually does his work by the book. He's not very inventive.

15. *call the shots*—have the authority in a situation; give orders

> We can give suggestions, but the boss calls the shots.
> Good parents don't let their children call the shots.

Check It Out

Take a closer look at the conversation from the "Zero In" section if you want to see any words or phrases that you might not have understood.

The Bad Driver

Driver: Yes, officer?

Policeman: Let me have your driver's license, please.

Driver: What did I do?

Policeman: Just give me your driver's license, sir.

Driver: But what did I do? Just tell me that.

Policeman: Sir, I'm just **going by the book**. First I get the driver's license, then I tell you what's wrong and write you a ticket. That's what the law tells me to do, and that's what I do.

Driver: Well, I don't want to give you my driver's license. What do you think about that?

Policeman: **According to** the law in this state, if you don't give me your driver's license, I can arrest you.

Driver: I didn't do anything wrong. OK, here. Here's my license.

Policeman: Do you realize you were driving 80 miles an hour in a 55 mile an hour area?

Driver: Ridiculous. What's the matter with you? Are you blind?

Policeman: I'd advise you not to **talk back**. You're in enough trouble already. In addition to speeding, your car was going crazy on the road. I think you're drunk, and that **calls for** a drunk driving test. Would you get out of your car, please?

---

* Punishments.

Driver: This is incredible. Do you know who I am?

Policeman: No, sir. Who are you?

Driver: I'm Judge Fonda's brother. Do you know Judge Fonda? He's one of the most important judges in the court system here.

Policeman: No, sir. I don't know **who's who** in the courts. There are too many judges in this area for me to know all of them. Besides, everybody tells me he can **pull strings**. Everybody says, "I know a judge and he'll fix everything." I don't believe it any more. Now I want you to walk 10 steps forward and 10 steps back.

Driver: When I tell my son the judge about this, he's really going to **put an end to** this terrible treatment of me. He'll stop it immediately. . . . There, I walked perfectly.

Policeman: No, sir, not perfectly. Now, breathe into this. . . . I'm afraid I'm going to have to arrest you for drunk driving.

Driver: Absolutely not. I refuse to go.

Policeman: It's not your decision to make. You don't **call the shots**. Get in.

Driver: Oh no. What am I going to do? Listen. I promise to **toe the line** in the future. I'll be good. I won't touch alcohol again. Let me go, please.

Policeman: It's too late for that now. We have to **go through proper channels**. I'll take you into the police station, we'll photograph you, and we'll take your fingerprints.

Driver: All that **red tape**? Why do we have to do all that paperwork? We don't really have to go to the police station, do we? I won't drink and drive again.

Policeman: You'll have to **take that up with** the judge. You can talk to the judge during your hearing, but I don't think your judge will be your brother.

Driver: What do you mean? Which judge will I have?

Policeman: Judge Horton. She'll **throw the book at** you when she sees the evidence. She might even send you to jail for a while.

Driver: That's not fair. She doesn't know me. I don't usually do this.

Policeman: Listen. We have to **crack down on** drunk driving, put people like you in jail. Too many people are dying because people like you "don't usually do this." And don't **get out of line** when you talk to the judge. If you cause too much trouble, you'll really have a big problem.

Understanding

6

"I can't make heads or tails of it."

Use this expression when you can't understand anything at all about something, when you can't even understand enough to know which part is the head and which part the tail. What can't you make heads or tails of in school, at work, or in your daily life? How can you learn to make heads or tails of it?

Get Ready

Prepare to hear a conversation by looking at the picture to the left and discussing the questions below with your teacher.

1. What is the relationship among these four people?
2. Where are they and what are they doing there?
3. Can you guess what they are talking about now?

Get the Gist

Answer these questions after you listen to the conversation one time.

The Best Way to Learn English

1. What method of learning English are the students discussing?
2. Do they think it's a good way?
3. What type of TV show does one speaker think is best for learning English?
4. Why does one speaker know so much about television news?

Zero In

Determine the meanings of this chapter's idioms by listening to the conversation again and circling the most likely meaning for each idiom.

1. *make out*	create	recognize	hear
2. *get*	understand	receive	tell
3. *figure out*	imagine	understand after examination	listen to
4. *catch on*	understand slowly	hold	receive
5. *fills me in*	brings inside	gives me permission	explains to me

6. *pick up on*	understand indirectly	choose	carry
7. *scratches the surface*	explains only a little	gives details	teaches
8. *got to the bottom of*	fell down	found all the information	emptied
9. *gather from*	collect	understand from information	steal
10. *make sense of*	earn money	write	find a way to understand
11. *read between the lines*	understand with little information	read poorly	not understand
12. *the ins and outs*	all of the details	both directly and indirectly	one part of the subject
13. *know the ropes*	am intelligent	understand the procedures	am careful
14. *dawned on*	was confusing	woke up	became understandable
15. *adds up*	is believable	is expensive	is difficult

Get Your Bearings

Use these exercises to become familiar with the idioms. You may want to refer to the definitions and examples at the end of this chapter while you do them.

Exercise 1: Write T if the statement is true and F if the statement is false.

_____ 1. An explanation that adds up is reasonable.

_____ 2. Most people want physicians who simply scratched the surface in medical school.

_____ 3. When you can't make out your telephone bill, it's a good idea to ask questions.

_____ 4. When you don't get a joke, you need someone to explain it.

_____ 5. People who pick up on things should be arrested.

_____ 6. A new employee isn't likely to know the ropes.

_____ 7. After a long absence or vacation, an employee needs to be filled in.

_____ 8. To get to the bottom of air pollution, we need to take an airplane.

_____ 9. People who read between the lines are poor readers.

_____ 10. If you learn the ins and outs of international relations, you'll have a lot of knowledge about the topic.

_____ 11. It's usually in the mornings when answers dawn on people.

_____ 12. A judge gathers from witnesses whether a person is guilty or innocent.

Exercise 2: Read the following paragraphs about Tina's learning problems. As you read, circle the idiom that better completes each sentence.

Ten-year-old Tina was always a poor student, and her parents were never able to **figure it out / know the ropes**. They accused Tina of not studying hard enough, yet they knew this reason only **added up / scratched the surface**. Finally, after worrying a long time, it **figured out / dawned on** them that Tina's problem might be very important. They took Tina to a psychologist to **get to the bottom of /gather from** the problem.

The psychologist, who was a learning specialist who **knew the ins and outs / added up** of learning disabilities, administered several tests to Tina. After 2 hours of testing, the psychologist **dawned on / gathered from** the evidence that Tina had a form of *dyslexia*. This means that when Tina reads, she is unable to **read between the lines / make sense** of the words because the letters in each word don't **fill in / add up** to whole words.

At the end of the session, the psychologist **made out / filled in** Tina's parents about the problem. The psychologist explained that research into learning disabilities is only just beginning—that educators don't always **know the ropes / add up** about correcting learning problems. But Tina's teachers can help her to read better by giving her exercises to do every day. In the beginning, the exercises will be hard, but Tina will soon **catch on to / dawn on** them. After some time, Tina will be able to **gather from / make out** words and sentences almost as easily as her friends do.

Exercise 3: Congratulations! You've been promoted to assistant editor of your newspaper. (Don't be too proud. There are many assistant editors.) As your first assignment, you've been told to "jazz up" (make more interesting) the headlines of the articles below. Use the idioms in the list to do this, and remember: headlines are supposed to be short but attention-getting. (Note: Sometimes, more than one headline is possible for an article. But use each only once.)

figure out	get to the bottom of	make sense of
catch on	scratch the surface	read between the lines
fill in	pick up on	
	add up	make out

1. _____   2. _____   3. _____

_____   _____   _____

(New York) Police today announced they have found a pattern to the bank robberies committed over the past 3 months. After studying the details of each robbery carefully, detectives began to notice

(Wash., D.C.) The attorney for the defense closed his arguments today by claiming the state does not have enough evidence to send his client to jail on charges of spying for other governments. "In my opinion," said Harold Barnes, "what they have doesn't equal a conviction for my client." His client, Marcia Wilde, is accused of passing unauthorized information to

(New Haven, Conn.) Researchers at Yale University have discovered one more possible cause of Alzheimer's disease. Acting on the hypothesis that a virus could lead to the neurological debilitation that is characteristic of the disease, they extracted white blood cells from the relatives of Alzheimer's patients and injected them into hamsters. Five of the 11 hamsters

4. _____

_____

(Ithaca, N.Y.) Astronomers at Cornell University have accidentally dicovered what may be the beginnings of a galaxy forming in an area that was, until now, empty. While checking their instruments, they detected radio waves in

5. _____

_____

(Miami) They had been receiving the messages for 14 months but could never understand them, despite the efforts of some of the government's most experienced "decoders." Now, with the help of world-renowned code-breaking expert Antonio Martelli, the U.S. Coast Guard not only knows the content of the messages, but can use

6. _____

_____

(Beijing) Calling the meeting between U.S. and Chinese representatives "a resounding success," the assistant secretary of state returns to Washington tomorrow to give details of the meeting to the president. While not being specific, the president has indicated a willingness to

7. _____

_____

(Pasadena, CA.) As Voyager 2 sends volumes of data to the Jet Propulsion Laboratory, astronomers here are only beginning their work: to understand all the information about this large planet and its eight moons. Scientists predict that they will need years to study the many

8. _____

_____

A new book can help parents deal with their children's lies. In *Why Kids Lie*, psychologist Paul Ekman explains how and why kids lie, as well as what parents should do about it. Until recently, most psychologists believed that young children didn't lie. But recent research shows that children lie for the same reasons as adults. For

9. _____

_____

Technology now offers us a wealth of possibilities in our everyday lives, but it hasn't even begun to affect us as much as it can. For example, genetic engineering now gives us fruit out of season and even combinations of fruit that wouldn't have occurred to our grandparents. But even now, genetic engineers are working on a tomato that stops ripening the moment it is picked and carrots that can stay crisp much longer

Ⓡ *Tune In*   Improve your ability to hear and understand idioms by listening to several short lectures and answering the questions below T for True or F for False.

A. (teenagers)

_____ *1.* The speaker believes teenagers are difficult to understand because their parents are not strict enough.

_____ *2.* The speaker believes that teenagers get into trouble because society treats them like adults even though they are really just children.

_____ *3.* According to the speaker, teenagers have a lot of problems because society has not given them a clear role to play.

_____ *4.* According to the speaker, teenagers and adults will probably never understand each other.

B. (jobs of the future)

_____ 5. People of the future are likely to think about time differently from the way people today think of time.

_____ 6. The speaker seems to believe that this new work method will make families stronger.

_____ 7. The speaker thinks this new work style could be harmful to businesses.

_____ 8. According to this passage, this new work style is likely to happen soon.

_____ 9. According to this passage, this new work style may be beneficial to children.

C. (nonverbal communication)

_____ 10. The speaker believes we can understand a person's intentions from his speech alone.

_____ 11. Most people understand nonverbal communication information about their own cultures without even thinking about it.

_____ 12. The rules of nonverbal communication are generally very similar from culture to culture.

Get Down to Business

Improve your ability to use this chapter's idioms in conversation with a couple of your classmates by acting out one or more of the roleplays below.

1. (newlyweds)

You've only been married a week, and already you're having your first big disagreement. (You decide what to disagree about. For example, did you agree to divide the housework 50/50 but now one of you isn't doing his or her share? Are you arguing about spending money? Does one of you want to spend all his or her time with friends and not enough time at home?)

Use the following idioms in your disagreement:

figure out	**get to the bottom of**	**fill someone in**
read between the lines	**add up**	**to get something**
	pick up on	**make out**
make sense of	**scratch the surface**	
catch on		

2. (a newlywed and a friend)

You've just had an argument with your new spouse. (You choose the topic.) Now you are talking about it with a good friend. It seems like your marriage is finished before it has even started. Your friend tries to give you good advice.

Use the following idioms during your discussion:

gather from	**figure out**	**know the ropes**
the ins and outs	**dawn on**	**scratch the surface**
fill someone in	**add up**	**get to the bottom of**
get	**catch on**	**read between the lines**

3. (2–3 friends)

You're all taking a tough course and having a terrible time understanding the subject matter. (You choose the course.) At first you complain about the class and the teacher to each other, but as you talk you start to see more hope for the future.

Use the following idioms during your conversation:

catch on	**make out**	**figure out**
to get something	**scratch the surface**	**make sense of**
fill someone in	**read between the lines**	**know the ropes**
the ins and outs		

4. (police officer and driving test taker)

You are taking your driving test today. You expect to pass the driving test easily, but you haven't studied much for the oral test. You don't want the officer to know that you haven't studied for the oral test. So every time the officer asks a question whose answer you don't know, you try to "buy time" by pointing out how unclearly it was explained in the study book or how confusing the question is. The officer, of course, soon realizes what you are doing and tries to make the questions extremely hard. Will you pass?

Use the following idioms during the test:

catch on to	**make out**	**figure out**
gather from	**know the ropes**	**scratch the surface**
to get something	**make sense of**	**read between the lines**
the ins and outs	**get to the bottom of**	

Put It All Together

Reinforce your ability to speak using many of the idioms you've learned so far by acting out one or more of the roleplays below with your classmates.

1. (2 or 3 friends from different countries)

You are in one person's country right now, but you are planning to travel to the other person's country. You want to know something about how to behave in the new country, so you ask your friend's advice about such things as following traffic signs, getting help from police and other authorities, spending your money wisely, bargaining when you buy things, and making friends.

Use the following idioms in your conversation:

catch on	**make out**	**figure out**
know the ropes	**the ins and outs**	**talk back**
who's who	**make ends meet**	**live it up**
go through proper channels	**bend over backwards to**	**take something up with someone**

2 (parents and parents-to-be)

Your good friends are about to be parents for the first time. You are all very excited about the news, but your friends are also worried about being good parents. As parents already, you are in a good position to give them advice on how to deal with children, finances, and keeping the relationship between husband and wife strong after the children arrive.

Use the following idioms during your discussion:

for good	**so far**	**fall through**
look forward to	**around the clock**	**take turns**
pull together	**give and take**	**help out**
do without	**be broke**	**know the ropes**
fill in	**the ins and outs**	**catch on**

3. (Psychiatrist and patient)

You've been having terrible nightmares every night for the past 3 weeks (you decide the details). They're driving you crazy! You've come to see the doctor to try to figure out what's causing them. Your psychiatrist studied in the Fraud school of psychiatry, where he learned that all human problems relate to money and power. By the way, your doctor charges $150 per hour, so hurry up!

Use the following idioms in your session:

make out	**add up**	**gather from**
get to the bottom of	**read between the lines**	**go by the book**
scratch the surface		**make a living by**
get out from under	**put an end to**	**talk back to**
who's who		**according to**

4. (3 housemates)

You live in a beautiful, turn-of-the-century home. This morning, some movie producers asked one of you to lend your house for their next Hollywood movie. The production company will pay a huge sum of money each day to use your house and plans to use it for 21 days. This sounds very exciting to you, but because you share ownership of the house with two other people, you have to tell them and get their permission when they come home. One of your housemates is worried that the movie company will harm the house. The other one is already planning how to spend the money.

Use the following idioms in your discussion:

fill in	**the ins and outs**	**read between the lines**
get out of line	**live it up**	
get out from under	**in the black**	**come up in the world**
help out	**call the shots**	**around the clock**
give a break	**figure out**	

Keep the Ball Rolling

Get still more practice with the idioms you've learned so far by participating in a discussion.

Imagine that you are a psychological counselor. People come to you to help them save their marriages, deal with their children, and set their lives straight (correct them). Read the following situations and discuss what you think each person's problem is and what advice you would give them.

Use the following idioms as you explain your advice for these problems:

#1	#2	#3
day in and day out	the ins and outs	day in and day out
for good	gather from	meet one halfway
around the clock	come up in the world	get to the bottom of
take turns	make a living by	bend over backwards to
bend over backwards to	in the long run	(all) add up
hand in hand	look forward to	scratch the surface
do without	carry out	make sense of
make ends meet	give a break	get out of line
dawn on	know the ropes	
add up	toe the line	
pick up on		

1. Mr. and Mrs. Petersen

Have been married for 9 years
Have 1 child, a son
They're both salespeople.
Having trouble making ends meet
His sick mother living with them for
the past year
They both travel a lot.
His parents are divorced.
Have been arguing a lot lately
Are considering divorce, but want
counseling first to try to save their
marriage

2. Todd Paley

26 years old
College graduate, BA psychology
Assistant manager of fast-food restau-
rant
Wants a better career; doesn't think
there's a future in this one
This is his first real job.
Enjoys the outdoors, travel, writing,
meeting new people, politics, read-
ing, and sports
Wants to earn a good salary
Doesn't like following other people's
rules

3. Tina Robard

15-year-old high school student
Has been moody and withdrawn lately
Has been skipping school
Stays in her bedroom all night listen-
ing to loud music
Has been looking pale and unhealthy
Has long, whispered telephone con-
versations with friends every night
Teachers complain about incomplete
work
Won't discuss problems with parents
Argues with parents and cries a lot
Parents are very worried; want to
know what to do

Put a Fine Point on Them

Use the following definitions and examples to help you understand the details of this chapter's idioms when you do the exercises.

1. *catch on (to something)*—understand after some time; realize

> Our boss was looking for ways to save money, but we didn't catch on, at first, that he might lay some of us off.
> I've finally caught on to Pat. He's not unfriendly, just shy.

2. *dawn on (someone)*—understand after some time; realize (compare with *catch on*) (uses inanimate subjects only)

> I sent Tim several letters, but he never answered them. It finally dawned on me that he never would.
> Margaret doesn't realize people are laughing at her. That fact will dawn on her in time.

3. *make out*—(S) recognize; understand from careful thought

> This might be where we turn. Can you make out the street sign?
> Once we made his handwriting out, we could follow his directions easily.

4. *(all) add up* (Int.)—be understandable; be sensible or believable (uses inanimate subjects only)

> It all adds up that Jan would want to be a corporate attorney. She's always loved finance.
> His explanation didn't add up even though he gave many details, so we couldn't approve his idea.

5. *figure out (something or someone)*—(S) understand after examination or thought; solve

> Can you figure out this map? I don't know where to go next.
> We'll have to figure Simmons' plans out if we're going to carry out the takeover of her company.

6. *gather from (something)*—understand based on information/evidence

> The government gathers from our records that we owe taxes.
> My physician gathered from my test results that I need surgery.

7. *get to the bottom of something*—understand the cause of a problem after investigation

> The doctors don't know why he's unconscious, but they've ordered tests to get to the bottom of it.
> Analysts haven't gotten to the bottom of the stock market crash yet.

8. *know the ropes*—understand a procedure or system

> Cindy didn't know the ropes when she started working at the newspaper. Now she's familiar with all the procedures.
> International students don't always know the ropes when they look for apartments.

9. *scratch the surface*—understand only a little, superficially

> We've scratched the surface today, but we're going to have to pull together to figure this problem out completely.
> Although scientists have been studying the universe for centuries, they've just scratched the surface.

10. *pick up on something*—understand intuitively, from indirect information; understand or discover without trying

> It's said that dogs and cats can pick up on human moods.
> Students pick up on their teachers' expectations and behave according to them.

11. *to get (something)*—to understand

> I don't get it. Why do we have to go to New York?
> Did you get that joke?

12. *fill in*—(S) give information; explain

> Jill doesn't know about the new regulation. I'll fill her in.
> Did you fill in your assistant about your change in schedule?

13. *make sense (out) of*—find a way to understand

> Can you make sense of this telephone bill?
> I made sense out of the computer manual but not the assignment.

14. *read between the lines*—understand from what hasn't been said

> The boss said he would do everything he could to save our jobs, but we could read between the lines. We'll probably be laid off.
> Your teacher said she appreciated your hard work, but she never said it was a good paper. Read between the lines!

15. *the ins and outs*—all the parts and their relationships (used with verbs of knowledge or understanding)

> Pat studied the ins and outs of airplanes before she could be an airplane mechanic.
> Studs Turkel has investigated the ins and outs of U.S. life.

Check It Out

Take a closer look at the conversation from the "Zero In" section if you want to see any words or phrases that you might not have understood.

The Best Way To Learn English

Luis: Do you ever try to learn English by watching TV?

Yukiko: Sometimes. But they talk so fast that I can't **make out** the words. It's much too hard to understand.

Xing: I know what you mean. I never **get** the jokes in the comedies. People in this country have a strange sense of humor.

Luis: But sometimes I can **figure out** some of the phrases and idioms, so I seem to be learning.

Yukiko: I had to watch TV here for weeks before I started to **catch on** to the pronunciation. Everyone speaks so fast on TV that I didn't know what I was listening to.

Giovanni: I'm lucky. I have an American roommate. When I don't understand something, he usually **fills me in**. He knows how to explain very clearly.

Xing: TV is good for learning English because I can sometimes **pick up on** the meaning of words by watching the people's faces or their actions.

Giovanni: I think listening to the news is the best way to learn English because news people speak more slowly and clearly.

Yukiko: Unfortunately, the news doesn't give many details. It only **scratches the surface**. I can't learn much about my country by watching the news.

Xing: That's right. Seong Kim told me there was a story about a problem in Korea last night. But he said it never **got to the bottom of** the problem. It didn't discuss all the causes or effects.

Luis: I'm taking a course now on mass media—newspaper, TV, and radio. I **gather from** the professor's lectures and the readings that TV stories are almost never detailed. Stories are usually only 10 or 15 seconds long.

Giovanni: Really? How can TV watchers **make sense of** such short stories? They must be awfully hard to understand.

Luis: You have to **read between the lines**. A lot of the information comes from the pictures—not the words.

Yukiko: Wow. You really seem to know **the ins and outs** of television news. How did you learn all this information, Luis?

Luis: My father works at a TV station in my country. That's why I'm studying it now. If I **know the ropes** when I return, he's promised to give me a job. But first I have to learn how TV functions.

Xing: Well, I think we should be out talking to people instead of watching TV.

Giovanni: That's really hard. Yesterday, I was waiting in line at the cafeteria. It seemed like an hour and I got angry. The guy behind me told me to "keep my shirt on." I had no idea what he meant. About 10 minutes later, the meaning **dawned on** me.

Yukiko: What does it mean?

Giovanni: "Be patient."

Luis: How did you figure that out?

Giovanni: From the situation. He wasn't angry. He was calm. Besides, I don't think he was interested in my shirt!

Xing: That **adds up**. You're very good at figuring out idioms, Giovanni.

Decisions

7

"I'll cross that bridge when I come to it."

This means, "I won't worry about making that decision or solving that problem until I absolutely have to." We use it when we want to postpone especially difficult decisions. Do you say something like this in your language? What bridge won't you cross until you come to it?

Get Ready

Prepare to hear a conversation by looking at the picture to the left and discussing the questions below with your teacher.

1. What is the man holding?
2. Does he look happy? What does he seem to be thinking about?
3. What do you think the woman is talking about?

Get the Gist

Answer these questions after you listen to the conversation one time.

School Decisions

1. Why hasn't the man registered for his courses yet?
2. What courses is he considering? What courses does he refuse to consider?
3. Why doesn't he want to ask the advisor to help him choose?

Zero In

Determine the meanings of this chapter's idioms by listening to the conversation again and circling the most likely meaning for each idiom.

1. *out of the question*	impossible	confusing	illegal
2. *make up my mind*	remember	decide	understand
3. *take into account*	pay for	remove	think about
4. *turned him down*	refused	walked away	gave him a low grade

5. *draw the line at*	fill out an application	not accept	stand in line
6. *looked over*	visited	found	studied carefully
7. *make a decision*	disagree	change	decide
8. *is up to you*	is your decision	is a problem for	needs time
9. *get rid of*	take another	add	remove
10. *on second thought*	after advice	after careful thought	after little thought
11. *change your mind*	think a long time	obey	make a different decision
12. *back out of*	change a decision	return	exit
13. *by all means*	of course	always	that's crazy
14. *have a voice in*	speak loudly	participate in a decision	give advice
15. *think twice about*	ask for help	not understand	consider carefully

Get Your Bearings

Use these exercises to become familiar with the idioms. You may want to refer to the definitions and examples at the end of this chapter while you do them.

Exercise 1: Write T if the sentence is true and F if it is false.

_____ *1.* When children misbehave, their parents should get rid of them.

_____ *2.* The best way to keep a good friend is to turn his invitations down often.

_____ *3.* If Tom asks his boss for a raise (more money) and his boss says "Out of the question," Tom might start planning how to spend the extra money.

_____ *4.* Whether or not a country has diplomatic relations with another country is probably up to the countries' leaders.

_____ *5.* Only unintelligent people have to think twice about things.

_____ *6.* One characteristic of a labor union is that it allows workers to have a voice in their company's management.

_____ *7.* A business person who backs out of a lot of deals will be well respected.

_____ *8.* It's a good idea to look a car over before buying it.

_____ *9.* The landlord said he draws the line at five roommates sharing an apartment. So my friend and I can start looking for three more roommates.

_____ *10.* When choosing a place to live, we have to take our budgets into account.

_____ *11.* I asked my mother whether I could live in the dormitory next year and she said, "By all means." This means I can start making plans to live there.

_____ *12.* You can't change your mind if you haven't made up your mind yet.

Exercise 2: Choose the correct idiom to complete each sentence.

1. This car is a real lemon.* I should have _____ more carefully before I bought it.

    a. changed my mind
    b. looked it over
    c. turned it down

2. Let's have our picnic right here, beside the barbecue grill. _____, let's go over there, by the river.

    a. Think twice about
    b. By all means
    c. On second thought

3. "Sir," said the store clerk, "I'll be happy to assist you after you've _____."

    a. made up your mind
    b. changed your mind
    c. taken into account

4. When Joan chose her apartment, she _____ how far it was from her job and her parents.

    a. got rid of
    b. made a decision
    c. took into account

5. To retaliate for the other country's actions, the president was willing to stop sending it food and to stop buying its exports, but she _____ declaring war against that country.

    a. out of the question
    b. drew the line at
    c. had a voice in

6. Bill wanted his parents to decide which college he should go to, but they told him the decision was _____.

    a. on second thought
    b. up to him
    c. by all means

* a bad car

7. The hospital is planning to allow the neighborhood around it to _____ the hospital's new expansion plans to prevent problems between the hospital and its neighbors.

    a. have a voice in
    b. get rid of
    c. make a decision

8. The mayor _____ the agreement with the investors after it became clear that most of the city's residents disapproved of the plan.

    a. changed her mind about
    b. backed out of
    c. turned down

9. Of course! _____, surprise them. They'll love it.

    a. By all means
    b. On second thought
    c. Out of the question

10. I can't believe that you've _____ such a wonderful deal. What was wrong with it?

    a. taken into account
    b. turned down
    c. looked over

11. Jamie's family is planning to travel to Europe early next month. But Jamie has a big examination at that time. He asked his teacher whether he could put it off or move it up, but the teacher, unfortunately, said that was _____.

    a. up to Jamie
    b. out of the question
    c. by all means

12. Tim and Sally never have any time alone because Tim's younger brother follows them everywhere. They're trying to think of a way to _____ him so they can watch TV alone.

    a. look over
    b. draw the line at
    c. get rid of

Exercise 3: You are a candidate in the election for mayor of your city. Your assistant has just given you a copy of the speech he wrote for you to deliver later this afternoon. Your opponent has accused you of being "weak and cold" when you speak in public. You want the speech to be more powerful, so you cross out the weak words and insert more vivid language (using the idioms in the list below).

think twice about	**on second thought**	**get rid of**
take into account	**made up my mind**	**up to us**

by all means	turn down	looked over
draw the line at	have a voice in	it's out of the question
back out of		

Today's Speech

Neighbors, this is my last speech before the election tomorrow, so I'd just like to summarize my position on the many issues before us.

Of course, any elected official must <u>consider</u> the children of our community when making plans. While I was out here campaigning, I <u>examined</u> some of our schools. Now, I have to admit, after I left the schools, I was pleased with them.

But <u>after thinking a while</u> I <u>decided</u> that we can do more. Our schools need bigger and better facilities, and it's <u>our decision</u>. We can have computer labs, swimming pools, and better audio-visual equipment in all our schools if we want them.

I also oppose building a new state prison facility in our community. We've worked very hard to <u>remove</u> the crime on our streets. If I'm elected mayor, I promise you I'll <u>refuse</u> any proposals to build a prison here. This is our community, and the state government shouldn't <u>have a role in</u> what kind of people live in our city. I have friends in high places, neighbors, and I promise you—they'll listen to me when I say, "<u>Absolutely not</u>."

Regarding the proposed subway linking downtown with the suburbs, I say to you, <u>of course</u>, build it. A subway system is certain to help our downtown businesses by giving all citizens easy access to downtown.

Of course, I promised to all of you not to raise your taxes, and I meant it.

There's no way that I'll <u>change that decision</u>. And despite the attacks my opponent has made against me on this point, I say to you that I do not need to <u>think again about</u> this. I have a great deal of experience with finances and budgeting. I won't have to <u>remove my support for</u> any of the promises I've made.

Tune In   Improve your ability to hear and understand idioms by listening to several conversations and answering the questions below T for True or F for False.

A. (husband and wife)

_____ *1.* The woman likes the picture.

_____ *2.* The man wants to put the picture in the bedroom.

_____ *3.* The woman agrees to put the picture in the bedroom.

B. (co-workers)

_____ 4. The woman's opinion about the contract seems to have changed.

_____ 5. The woman finally agrees to the contract.

C. (co-workers)

_____ 6. The company approved the speakers' request.

_____ 7. The speakers plan to continue trying.

_____ 8. The speakers probably asked for more money.

D. (student and teacher)

_____ 9. Tim isn't happy with Dr. Henderson's decision.

_____ 10. Dr. Henderson didn't consider Tim's excuse.

E. (friends)

_____ 11. Both friends will go to the concert.

_____ 12. One of the speakers will pay someone to accept a package.

Get Down to Business

Improve your ability to use this chapter's idioms in conversation with a couple of your classmates by acting out one or more of the roleplays below.

1. (2 roommates OR a new husband and wife)

You are looking for a new apartment, and this is the sixth apartment you've looked at today. You're starting to get tired and a little bit angry with each other because you can't seem to agree on anything. The apartment you are looking at now is very nice and priced right. One of you seems willing to take anything as long as it's warm, dry, and comfortable. The other one, the "picky" one, has a lot of requirements about size, location of rooms with respect to the sun, closet space, convenience of the kitchen, etc. At first, you both agree that the apartment is nice, but soon the "picky" person begins to notice problems and, once again, it looks like this apartment won't be adequate.

Use the following idioms in your argument:

take into account	turn down	draw the line at
look over	be up to	change one's mind
out of the question	on second thought	think twice about
make a decision	have a voice in	make up one's mind

2. (a bride and 2 bridesmaids OR a groom and 2 groomsmen)

You are about to get married in less than 30 minutes and you're starting to change your mind. Who IS this person you're going to marry, anyway? What about his or her terrible habits? Will you lose all of your independence after you get married? Why spoil a perfectly happy life by getting married?

Your bridesmaids or groomsmen (friends who participate in the ceremony) realize that you only have the premarriage "jitters" (nervousness). They try to convince you that everything is OK and your decision to marry is a good one.

Use the following idioms as you talk:

make up one's mind	**turn down**	**draw the line at**
out of the question	**be up to someone**	**by all means**
change one's mind	**on second thought**	**think twice about**
back out of	**have a voice in**	**make a decision**
take into account	**get rid of**	

3. (a used car salesperson, a customer, and a family member)

A week ago, you bought a used car from this salesperson. Since you bought it, you've had nothing but trouble with it. It's clear to you that the salesperson sold you a "lemon." Now you want your money back. You believe that companies have an obligation to back up their products. You threaten to go to court when the salesperson refuses your request.

The salesperson refuses to accept the car or give you your money back. He or she says you were told that none of the cars had guarantees when you bought your car, and if you didn't test-drive the car enough, that's your problem, not the company's. It is not the company's policy to allow cars to be returned. The sales person doesn't own the company.

Use the following idioms in your argument:

get rid of	**take into account**	**turn down**
draw the line at	**out of the question**	**be up to someone**
look over	**think twice about**	**back out of**
have a voice in	**make a decision**	**on second thought**

4. (2–3 friends)

Your city is going to have an election soon, and you and your friends are discussing who you think should win. The candidates are:

a. Sandy Mooney: (female) 46 years old, a college graduate, was director of the city's urban planning department for the past 12 years and is the current mayor, is married with three teenaged children, is known to be rather liberal. *Supports* child care, increased school budget, and new subway system. *Opposes* increase in taxes to fund subway system.

b. Arnold Shumway: (male) 57 years old, 8th grade education, has never worked in city government, believes all politicians are controlled by radio waves from outer space.

c. Paul Antonelli: (male) 50 years old, 2 years of college, has been city financial director for the past 6 years, is married with four grown children, is known to be a moderate. *Supports*: tax breaks for businesses to increase business growth in city, city-funded college scholarships. *Opposes*: businesses providing child care, new subway system, increased school budget.

Use the following idioms in your discussion:

get rid of	**make up one's mind**	**take into account**
out of the question	**be up to**	**look over**
on second thought	**think twice about**	**have a voice in**
make a decision about	**draw the line at**	**by all means**

Put It All Together

Reinforce your ability to speak using many of the idioms you've learned so far by acting out one or more of the roleplays below with your classmates.

1. (up to 4 family members)

You and several members of your family are planning a 50th anniversary party for your parents. You want this to be a very special occasion to mark what you, your cousins, aunts, and uncles consider to be a very special marriage. You must discuss the time, location, cost, music, food, etc. You'd especially like to use a certain restaurant, but it can be very hard to get because it's so popular. You don't want this to be a cheap event, but none of you is rich either. Everyone will contribute a certain amount of money to finance the party.

Use the following idioms as you discuss the party:

ahead of time	**for the time being**	**keep track of**
give a hand	**come through for**	**live it up**
run	**break even**	**run out of**
pull strings	**fill someone in**	**figure out**
take into account	**have a voice in**	**turn down**
out of the question	**draw the line at**	**be up to someone**

2. (3 friends)

One of you has had a job that you haven't been happy with for about 2 years. There doesn't seem to be much opportunity for growth in this job anymore and you've been bored. But you can't make a decision. (In the U.S., changing jobs is often considered necessary for professional growth.) For one thing, your job is secure: it has a certain amount of prestige and it provides you with a pretty good income. But you can't help wondering what job might be out there that could maximize your potential. You're thinking about quitting now so that you can spend all your time looking for something better. Your friends are questioning you and offering you their advice.

Use the following idioms in your discussion:

for the time being	**in the long run**	**right away**
in time	**so far**	**put off**
carry out	**land on one's feet**	**be broke**
gather from	**take into account**	**think twice about**
make a decision	**be up to someone**	**draw the line at**

3. (3 friends)

All of you are planning to take a wonderful vacation together. You have brochures from several great places (you decide which). You are discussing the advantages and disadvantages of each. One of you, however, is rather shy. You find it difficult to state your opinion strongly, so the others don't appear to be listening to you very much.

Use the following idioms in your discussion (those in brackets [] are especially appropriate if you plan a vacation in another country):

take into account	**draw the line at**	**have a voice in**
by all means	**look over**	**run (cost)**
live it up	**be a steal**	**take turns**
just around the corner	**ahead of time**	**go broke**
on the spur of the moment	**[get out of line]**	**[red tape]**
	[toe the line]	**[know the ropes]**

4. (2 or 3 friends)

You've fallen in love with two people. You are at a time in your life when you want to "settle down," get married, and start having children. But you can't decide which person you want to marry. One of them is very wealthy and has a powerful family. This could be very helpful in your career and your future would be easy. The other one is very poor but a very helpful person. This person is always willing to spend time with you to advise you about any problems you may have in your work or personal life. This person makes your life easy in a different way, more comfortable. You think both would be happy to marry you.

Discuss your problem with your friend(s) using the following idioms:

take into account	**make up one's mind**	**change one's mind**
pull strings	**call the shots**	**come up in the world**
live it up	**get out from under**	**bend over backwards to**
who's who	**right-hand woman or man**	**give and take**
pull together	**help out**	
make ends meet		

Keep the Ball Rolling

Get still more practice with the idioms you've learned so far by participating in a discussion.

Among some people in the U.S., it's becoming popular to have something called a prenuptial contract—an agreement, written and signed before the marriage, that details how all the money and property will be divided if the couple divorces or one spouse dies.

Imagine that you are a lawyer or a parent of the couples described below. Do you think these couples should have prenuptial contracts? Why or why not? After your discussion, explain who might need a prenuptial contract.

Use the following idioms when you explain your decisions:

in the long run	**in time**	**fall through**
call off	**give-and-take**	**pull together**
call for	**change one's mind**	**back out of**
take into account	**think twice about**	**get rid of**
draw the line at	**out of the question**	**call the shots**
read between the lines		

Couple #1

Steven Palmer

33 years old
Physician: surgeon
Divorced
No children
Earned $123,000 last year

Janet Cooper

29 years old
Lawyer
Never married
Earned $63,000 last year
Job requires her to travel a lot

Couple #2

Martha Worthington

56 years old
Widow
Three grown children
Inherited several million dollars on husband's death
Men can receive alimony* in her state

Roger Horton

46 years old
Previously married, a widower
An actor, not very famous
Is not poor, but has little money
Has been seeing Martha for almost 2 years

* Money given by one spouse to another, after a divorce, for living expenses.

Couple #3

Robert Harrison   **Nicole Howard**

24 years old   20 years old
Graduated college 2 years   High school graduate
   ago   Comes from rather wealthy
Son of a very wealthy   family
   industrial family   Parents are very pleased
The business has always   about the upcoming
   been in the family; Robert   marriage.
   has worked in it for 6 years.   Parents divorced when she
Has known Nicole since he   was 12.
   was a child   Has never been employed;
                             does volunteer work on a
                             few committees

Put a Fine Point on Them

Use the following definitions and examples to help you understand the details of this chapter's idioms when you do the exercises.

1. *get rid of*—remove; send or throw away

   I have to get rid of my car. I can't afford to keep it.
   Oh no, Bill's at the door. Get rid of him.

2. *make up (one's) mind (about something)*—decide

   I can't make up my mind about whether to go to Florida or California for my vacation.
   Make up your mind! Do you want to go to a movie or go bowling?

3. *take into account*—(S) consider when making a decision

   When Joanne decided on her college, she took into account its reputation and location.
   You should take your personality and talents into account when choosing a career.

4. *turn down*—(S) refuse; reject

   He turned down a piece of cake after eating a whole pizza.
   I applied for the job, but they turned me down.

5. *draw the line at*—not accept (+ V + ing or + N indicating the thing that's unacceptable)

   I like basketball, but I draw the line at watching four games in a row.
   Mr. Morris wants to win the election very much, but he draws the line at a lot of trips without his family.

6. *out of the question*—absolutely impossible

   A long vacation is out of the question this year. How about next year?
   Friday looks out of the question for the staff meeting. Let's do it Monday.

7. *be up to (someone)*—be the decision of someone

   The location of the new playground is up to the City Council.
   Do you want to go to the Swanson's party or stay home? It's up to you.

8. *change (one's) mind (about something)*—change one's decision or opinion

   I was going to stay home, but I've changed my mind.
   Steve and Carla changed their minds about having their wedding next
     month because there won't be enough time to prepare.

9. *look over*—(S) examine carefully; study

   I need time to look these papers over before I sign them.
   People usually look over a lot of apartments before they sign a lease.

10. *on second thought*—change a decision after thinking about it again

    Let's go see a movie. . . . On second thought, let's stay home. I'm too tired
      to go out.
    Ms. Jackson almost fired her clerk for his mistake, but, on second thought,
      she only suspended him for 2 weeks.

11. *think twice (about)*—think very carefully about a difficult decision (+ V +
    ing) (not think twice about = have an easy decision)

    If you think an apartment above a restaurant is a good idea, you'd better
      think twice.
    Joe didn't think twice about joining the circus. He'd dreamed about it all
      his life.

12. *back out (of)*—change a decision or agreement that has already been made;
    remove support for a decision

    Martha agreed to have the operation but, at the last minute, became afraid
      and backed out of it.
    Linda backed out of the law partnership when she was offered a better deal
      at another firm.

13. *have a voice in*—have a role in decision-making

    Parents want to have a voice in their children's educations.
    Many U.S. citizens don't have a voice in their government because they
      don't vote.

14. *make a decision (about)*—decide; choose

    Did you make a decision about the apartment on Fifth Avenue? Will you
      take it?
    I can't make a decision. Three universities have accepted me and they're all
      very good.

15. *by all means*—certainly; of course

    By all means, you should stay in California for at least 2 weeks. You'll really
      enjoy yourself.
    You want to borrow my pen? By all means; here it is.

Check It Out

Take a closer look at the conversation from the "Zero In" section if you want to
see any words or phrases that you might not have understood.

School Decisions

Alice: Have you decided what courses you're going to take next semester?

Ben: So far, it looks like I'm taking seven courses.

Alice: You can't do that. That's **out of the question**. It's too many courses to take at the same time.

Ben: I know. But I can't **make up my mind**. I want to take Spanish, but I also like French and German.

Alice: You should **take into account** the usefulness of each language. Spanish is very useful in the United States, so that's an important consideration.

Ben: Yes, but the class is already closed.

Alice: Then it's impossible, right?

Ben: No, I could ask for special permission to register.

Alice: Good idea.

Ben: But a friend of mine asked for permission and the teacher **turned him down**. Now he has to find a different class too.

Alice: You know, I've always wanted to study Arabic or Chinese. Why don't we do it together?

Ben: Absolutely not. I **draw the line at** languages with difficult writing systems.

Alice: OK. What else are you planning to study?

Ben: I need a science class, but I don't know which one.

Alice: Have you **looked over** the schedule of courses?

Ben: Sure, but I can't **make a decision**.

Alice: Well, only you can decide. Your schedule **is up to you**, not me.

Ben: I think I have to **get rid of** a couple of courses. Maybe I should take out the language and sciences classes.

Alice: What else do you have there?

Ben: English, math, history, psychology, and music. **On second thought**, maybe I should take Spanish instead of math.

Alice: You know, you can **change your mind** later. You don't have to make the final decision now. If you aren't happy with your choices after the semester starts, you can **back out of** some of the courses.

Ben: That's true. Maybe I should take mathematics. It's important.

Alice: **By all means**. Everyone needs mathematics.

Ben: I'm so confused about this. I think I'll have to talk to my advisor.

Alice: That's a good idea. He can help you figure out what to register for.

Ben: The problem is that he never lets me **have a voice in** my registration when I ask for his help. He tries to make the decision for me without asking my opinion.

Alice: Yeah. I know what you mean. Then you'd better **think twice about** going to him for help. It might not be a very good idea.

Opportunity

8

"Strike while the iron is hot."

This means that we should take an opportunity quickly, before it disappears. It refers to making iron objects such as horseshoes by heating the iron and beating it into shape before it becomes cool. When might someone have to strike while the iron is hot? Is it common in your culture to take opportunities quickly?

Get Ready

Prepare to hear a conversation by looking at the picture to the left and discussing the questions below with your teacher.

1. What is in the man's case? Why do you think he's carrying these things?
2. Does he seem to be happy?
3. Why do you think the woman is on the telephone?

Get the Gist

Answer these questions after you listen to the conversation one time.

Job Prospects

1. What kind of job does the man have now?
2. Why isn't he successful at this job?
3. Do you think he is an intelligent person and a good problem solver?
4. What does the woman suggest?
5. What is the man going to do next? Do you think he'll succeed?

Zero In

Determine the meanings of this chapter's idioms by listening to the conversation again and circling the most likely meaning for each idiom.

1. *have what it takes*	be rich	be happy	be qualified
2. *get cold feet*	become afraid	become cold	become sick
3. *make good*	be creative	succeed	have fun

4. *strike out*	hit someone	fail	try something new
5. *not stand a chance*	not be possible	wait a long time	be lucky
6. *break into*	steal	begin	disturb
7. *have a lot going for*	have advantages	lose a lot	travel a lot
8. *get ahead*	go too fast	become more successful	become happier
9. *get to*	receive	have the opportunity	want
10. *up for grabs*	available	stolen	far away
11. *jumped at*	was surprised	ran away	quickly accepted
12. *might as well*	should not	it's a good idea	it's ridiculous
13. *play it by ear*	not be serious	listen carefully	do without planning
14. *miss out on*	lose an opportunity	feel homesick	get lost
15. *miss the boat*	arrive too late	lose an opportunity to travel	be very angry

Get Your Bearings

Use these exercises to become familiar with the idioms. You may want to refer to the definitions and examples at the end of this chapter while you do them.

Exercise 1: Read each statement and write T if it's true or F if it's false.

_____ 1. A person who misses the boat will have to find another form of transportation or swim.

_____ 2. Most employers want to hire employees who have something going for them.

_____ 3. If you have what it takes to complete a program at a university, the university should accept your application.

_____ 4. A person jumps at a suggestion when he is insulted by it.

_____ 5. A short person with bad eyesight probably doesn't stand a chance of being a great basketball player.

_____ 6. If someone takes something that is up for grabs, he should be arrested.

_____ 7. People who play situations by ear probably like to do things on the spur of the moment too.

_____ 8. A father and mother can be proud of a child who makes good.

_____ 9. A child who misses out on a party might cry.

_____ 10. Nowadays it's probably a good idea to break into a high-technology field.

_____ *11.* If you don't want to take a dance class, you might as well study ancient Greek.

_____ *12.* Armies especially want soldiers who get cold feet when they fight.

_____ *13.* If Joe says, "I get to cook dinner for everyone on Saturday," he's happy about it.

_____ *14.* If you strike out on several mathematics tests, your grade will be very good.

_____ *15.* One way to get ahead is by getting a college degree.

Exercise 2: Fill in the blanks with the correct idiom from the list below.

struck out	**have a lot going for**	**missed the boat**
getting cold feet	**jumped at**	**make good**
up for grabs	**might as well**	**play it by ear**
	got to	

1. "Mommy!" the little boy said excitedly. "I _____ touch the horse's nose!"

2. "You shouldn't be so upset, Jan. You'll find another job. You _____ _____ yourself. You're clever and hardworking."

3. "Oh, no. I think I'm _____. I can't go out there and talk to all of those people. I'm too nervous."

4. "Mark, didn't you say you were looking for another apartment? There's one _____ in my building. Here's the telephone number."

5. "Nobody ever expected him to _____. When he was young, he was always in trouble, never went to school. We all felt sorry for his parents. Now he's doing so well"

6. "Harvard's offered a full scholarship to Cathy. Of course, she _____ the chance to go to Harvard. Who wouldn't?"

7. "Sure I'm nervous about meeting my in-laws.* John wanted to give me some information about what to talk about, but I'd rather _____."

8. The students tried to convince the teacher to put off the big examination, but they _____. The test is tomorrow.

9. The President really _____ by not scheduling a meeting with the visiting leader. No solution to our problems can be found without discussing them together.

10. "Your car is in the mechanic's shop so often that you _____ not have a car at all. Take the bus!"

---

* The family of one's husband or wife.

Exercise 3: You are Ronald Rump, a very wealthy, powerful, no-nonsense businessman. When you want something, you want it yesterday. This morning, you asked your large staff to do research and prepare recommendations on ten opportunities for your business conglomerate.

Now you have their report in front of you and you will scribble your comments after each recommendation, using the idioms below (you're a businessman of few words!). (Because some idioms have approximately the same meaning, more than one comment may be possible.)

Play it by ear!	**We struck out!**	**I'll miss out on ____!**
We missed the boat!	**Let's break into it!**	**We might as well!**
She has what it takes!	**It doesn't stand a chance!**	**They got cold feet!**
Jump at it!	**He won't get ahead in law!**	

Summary of Business Opportunities

Example: *Your son*
Your son has been working as an assistant in the law department for 2 years. He still hasn't passed his law examination and he's not helping much in the law department. Can we put him somewhere else?

Yeah. He won't get ahead in law!

1. *Purchase of D.D.O., Inc.*
Cost was $62 million, now $96 million. Other buyers are interested. It was a much better deal last year.

2. *Diversification of our Enterprises*
Right now, we have holdings in energy, banking, and construction. The electronics field is growing fast. We should move to acquire some electronics firms.

3. *Sale of our Icelandic fish factory*
Loses a lot of money every year; Equipment is too old-fashioned. Workers prefer traditional methods. Do you think we can find a buyer for it?

4. *Establishing political support*
You have a meeting with the governor next month. You need to convince him to sign the new tax law. We have a large staff gathering

evidence for your meeting. I can get a speech writer to prepare a statement for you. We can plan everything you have to say, to the last detail. Do you want this?

5. *Appointing a new vice president of finance*
One applicant seems possible. She has an M.B.A. from Wharton, 10 years' experience as financial analyst on the New York Stock Exchange, 5 years' experience with the top brokerage in the nation. Her interviews went very well. What do you think?

6. *B. B. Green's attempt to get control of our oil refinery*
They had 12% of our stock. But when the price of the stock went up so fast, they sold it. We can't make it out. They were winning. What happened?

7. *The Clay Department Store chain*
The chain is up for grabs. Its owner needs cash, so he's selling it cheaply. The chain is a great money-maker. Current employees can stay in place. We don't see any disadvantages at all. What do you say?

8. *Merger of our banks with Transcontinental*
Negotiations were slow, lots of areas of disagreement. Before negotiations concluded, Transcon merged with First South Bank. Afraid we lost that one.

9. *Talk with the U.S. President*
The only time we could get for you with the President was Friday at 3 p.m. Unfortunately, your son is getting married at the same time. Do you still want to meet the President?

10. *Option to purchase building*
Prime location in Chicago, great condition, good-looking, cheap. Can be converted to apartments or hotel. Should we buy it? Great money-maker.

Tune In

Improve your ability to hear and understand idioms by listening to several conversations and answering the questions below T for True or F for False.

A. (a student and his advisor)

_____ *1.* Sam wants to major in mathematics.

_____ *2.* Sam's advisor thinks he should major in information science.

_____ *3.* Sam didn't do well in his last math class.

_____ *4.* Sam didn't make a decision about his major by the end of the conversation.

B. (a husband and wife)

_____ *5.* The wife is sure her husband will like her news.

_____ *6.* The wife received the new job because she asked for it.

_____ *7.* The wife's new job will be in another city.

_____ *8.* The husband thinks his wife should take the new job.

_____ *9.* The husband and wife have moved at least one time already.

C. (two friends)

_____ *10.* Pat prepared very carefully for the interview.

_____ *11.* Pat has a good singing voice but no experience.

_____ *12.* Pat became so frightened that she went home before her interview.

_____ *13.* Pat wasn't surprised that she got the job.

_____ *14.* Pat's friend, Chris, is jealous of Pat.

Get Down to Business

Improve your ability to use this chapter's idioms in conversation with a couple of your classmates by acting out one or more of the roleplays below.

1. (2–3 friends)

You are all discussing the state "lottery," a contest run by the state government in which participants buy tickets with their favorite numbers on them for a dollar or more. The government uses a machine to choose a winning number randomly. Winners can sometimes win as much as $20 million or more.

One or two of you plays the lottery every day or every week, depending on the game (and there are many types of games). You are trying to convince your friends to do the same because they can become rich, and the profit the government makes goes to charity.

The other one or two of you thinks playing the lottery is nothing more than gambling, a practice you disapprove of. You believe your friends' behavior is immoral and you are angry at your government for condoning it.

Argue about the lottery using the following idioms:

miss the boat	**strike out**	**be up for grabs**
get to (+ V)	**miss out on**	**might as well**
(not) stand a chance	**get ahead**	**play by ear**
make good	**have something going for one**	**jump at**

2. (2–3 friends and a famous person)

You and your friends are having dinner in an elegant restaurant, an unusual treat for all of you because you are not wealthy people. Suddenly, you recognize a celebrity all of you have admired for a long time, someone who hasn't been seen in public for nearly 20 years. (You decide who it is!) You'd really like to talk to the celebrity, and discuss it with each other first. Then you go over and talk. (What's the celebrity's reaction?)

Use the following idioms in your conversations:

miss the boat	**strike out**	**get cold feet**
get to (+ V)	**miss out on**	**might as well**
jump at	**play by ear**	**stand a chance**
by all means	**out of the question**	**draw the line at**

3. (student and parent[s])

You'll be graduating from high school this spring and going to college in the fall. You've been accepted by several local colleges, all good schools. Yesterday, you received a full scholarship offer from a university in another country. It is a very prestigious school, especially for the field you want to study (you choose the field). Everyone who goes to that school goes on to do important things with his or her life. The problem is that you're nervous about living in another country, so far from your family. Your parents have always supported what you want to do, but they're a little worried too.

Discuss this with your parents using the following idioms:

make good	**miss the boat**	**get cold feet**
get to	**miss out on**	**jump at**
get ahead	**might as well**	**play by ear**
have something going for one	**have what it takes**	
	be up for grabs	

4. (a husband and wife)

One of you has been offered two different jobs. The first job does not pay much money and has little status associated with it, but it offers a lot of variety (which means it won't be boring), it will use all of your creative talents, and it will allow you to work with and help people. The hours are flexible and often require working overtime. There's not much possibility of advancement in this job.

The second job pays much more money and has a higher status, but it is rather routine, requires you to work in an office most of the time, and gives you a chance to help people only very indirectly. This is a 9:00 to 5:00 job only. It's possible to advance in this job. (You decide what each particular job should be.) Discuss which job will provide the best opportunity for you and your family.

Use the following idioms in your discussion:

have what it takes	**get to**	**miss out on**
jump at	**get ahead**	**might as well**
be up for grabs	**make good as**	**not stand a chance of**

Put It All Together

Reinforce your ability to speak using many of the idioms you've learned so far by acting out one or more of the roleplays below with your classmates.

1. (2–4 friends)

You have been working as an investment banker for the past 8 years, and you're very unhappy about it. All your life you've lived and worked in brick and glass buildings, with machines and artificial light. You have come to believe that human beings were never meant to live this way. You want to "get back to nature." You're planning to quit your job and buy a farm. You believe that you were always meant to be a farmer, and it's time to correct the mistake. Your friends think you are crazy to throw away a great job for something you know nothing about.

Use the following idioms in your discussion with your friends:

miss the boat	**make good as**	**strike out**
have what it takes	**not stand a chance**	**play by ear**
make up one's mind	**get rid of**	**back out of**
catch on to	**the ins and outs**	**go broke**
on the spur of the moment	**day in and day out**	**carry out**

2. (up to 5 extended family members)

You are at a family reunion with nearly a hundred members of your extended family (including aunts, uncles, cousins, etc.). At this moment, you are speaking to a few family members. None of you has seen each other in at least a year (longer if some of you didn't attend the reunion last year).

A. One of you has lost his job and is planning to move to Arizona to find another job. Your spouse and children aren't happy about this, but it's the only choice.

B. Two of you have started a business together. It's not completely successful yet, but it looks like it will be very successful in the future.

C. One of you always wanted to be a physician, but money was short (not enough) so you became a physician's assistant instead. You still hope to go to medical school one day, but now you're older and afraid your educational background is not good enough.

D. Everyone always thought you would be a famous singer, but you've never had the nerve (been brave enough) to go to an entertainment capital like London or Los Angeles and try.

Use the following idioms as you talk:

strike out	have what it takes	get cold feet
might as well	jump at	play by ear
get rid of	change one's mind	make a decision
fall through	come through for	bend over backwards to
for the time being	get out from under	
come up in the world	pull together	pull together
miss out on	get ahead	break into
make good	have what it takes	pull strings

3. (2–3 colleagues)

Your city is governed by a city council—a group of representatives from all parts of the city who work with the mayor on city issues such as budgets and lawmaking. The next election is in one year, and your colleagues are trying to convince you to run because you support air pollution control. Your city has several factories that pollute the air terribly. Pollution control is crucial, in your opinion. You have never before considered running for public office, but the more you discuss it with your colleagues, the surer you are that you could do a good job. Your colleagues believe that you have a good chance of winning because you can raise enough money and because there are a lot of people who like and respect you.

Use the following idioms in your discussion:

have what it takes	jump at	break into
be up for grabs	might as well	have a voice in
make sense of	add up	stand a chance
put an end to	call the shots	come through for
just around the corner	throw the book at	

4. (2 friends)

A friend of yours was going to take a fantastic trip with another friend next week. But the other friend got sick. Now your friend is offering the trip to you instead, at no cost to you. (You choose the place.) You're very excited, of course; you've always wanted to go there but never thought you'd be able to. But you're worried that you can't get time off from work so soon or be able to prepare so quickly. Your friend promises to help.

Use the following idioms in your conversation:

jump at	**be up for grabs**	**get to**
(not) miss out on	**live it up**	**give a hand**
go through proper channels	**look forward to**	**back out of**
	take something up with someone	**be up to**
on the spur of the moment		

Keep the Ball Rolling Get still more practice with the idioms you've learned so far by participating in a discussion.

Jann and Mark Rice have been living in North Belmont for the past 12 years. They have two children, Amy, 10; and Mark, Jr., 8. Mark is a chemistry professor for a large, urban university. Jann is a regional sales manager for a computer firm. Jann earns a few thousand dollars less than Mark does. Last week, Jann's boss offered her a promotion. Her new job would have much more responsibility and much more money—about 30% more. However, Jann would be required to move 1,100 miles away from North Belmont. The family must now consider three options:

1. Jann accepts the job and the whole family moves.
2. Jann accepts the job and travels home on weekends.
3. Jann refuses the job and keeps her present job.

Imagine that you are a friend or relative, and the Rices have asked your advice. What do you think the Rice family should do? What elements enter into your decision?

Use the following idioms when you present the results of your discussion:

miss the boat	**get to**	**miss out on**
might as well	**stand a chance**	**get ahead**
play by ear	**break into**	**make good**
take into account	**draw the line at**	**think twice about**
make ends meet	**do without**	**live it up**
make a living by	**back out of**	**put an end to**
look forward to	**hand in hand**	**bend over backwards to**
for good		

Now, imagine that Mark were offered the promotion in New York, with the accompanying increase in responsibility and money. Would your decision change?

Put a Fine Point on Them

Use the following definitions and examples to help you understand the details of this chapter's idioms when you do the exercises.

1. *miss the boat*—lose an opportunity

   Joyce, you really missed the boat. Ann was looking for a roommate to share her apartment, but she found one while you were out of town.

   I wanted to see the movie that won three Academy Awards, but I missed the boat when it left town before I could.

2. *make good (as something)*—succeed

   Everybody always thought of Todd as a failure. But after he graduated from college and left town, he surprised everybody by making good in New York.

   Since Sharon has already made good as a magazine writer, she wants to try writing scripts for television.

3. *strike out*—fail (past tense, *struck*) (comes from baseball: three strikes and the player is out)

   Bob tried to meet his beautiful new neighbor in the laundry room, but he struck out.

   Scientists have been looking for a cure for the common cold, but so far they've struck out.

4. *have (something) going for (one)*—have an advantage or benefit

   Cliff is short for a basketball player, but he has a few things going for him. He's fast and very smart.

   Loretta has a lot going for her. She's smart, energetic, and well-educated.

5. *have what it takes*—be qualified, capable (+ to + V)

   The new president has what it takes to lead the country.

   Johnny says he wants to do well in this course, but he just doesn't have what it takes. He should try something else.

6. *get cold feet (about something)*—become so afraid that one can't do something

   Rick wanted to take his driving test yesterday, but he got cold feet about the written exam and didn't go.

   I've made six appointments with my dentist, but I always get cold feet.

7. *get to*—have a welcome opportunity (+ to + V)

   Did you get to see the White House when you were in Washington?

   I never get to drive the car when we go on long trips.

8. *miss out (on something)*—lose an opportunity

   Bill missed out on the marathon, but he's looking forward to the bicycle race in June.

   The real estate agent told us we missed out on the colonial house on the corner. It was sold yesterday.

9. *jump at (something)*—make immediate use of an opportunity

   I would jump at a trip around the world, wouldn't you?

   My grandmother jumped at the chance to visit Elvis Presley's home. She's always loved him and his music.

10. *(not) stand a chance*—have a good opportunity or possibility (usually used in the negative or questions) (of + V ing)

   Todd doesn't stand a chance of finding a ride home after the party. He lives too far away.

   Does Lisa stand a chance of getting an apartment? I thought they were all taken.

11. *get ahead* (Int.)—become more successful; get a job promotion

   You'll get ahead if you work hard.

   Jack got ahead by being friendlier with his boss.

12. *break into*—begin a project or career successfully

   Yolan was young when she broke into the newspaper business.

   It's hard to break into films unless you're already an established actor.

13. *be up for grabs*—be available to take

   The job was up for grabs, but nobody applied for it.

   Many scholarships are up for grabs each year, but nobody applies for them.

14. *might as well*—a good idea; equal or preferable to the alternative (+ V)

   Karen was thinking about finding a new apartment. But her present apartment, though small, is pretty cheap. She might as well stay there.

   I'm never going to learn English. I might as well quit.

15. *play (something) by ear*—deal with a situation as it happens, without planning

   Jeff doesn't like to prepare for job interviews. He prefers to play them by ear. He believes he can be more creative in his answers that way.

   Because the reporter didn't have time to prepare her interview of the vice president, she had to play it by ear.

Check It Out

Take a closer look at the conversation from the "Zero In" section if you want to see any words or phrases that you might not have understood.

Job Prospects

Tony: I've got to find a new job.

Janet: What's wrong with the job you have now?

Tony: I'm a terrible salesperson. I don't **have what it takes**. I don't like talking to strangers, and I don't like the product I have to sell. Every time I have to go to another office to make a sale, I **get cold feet**.

Janet: What do you mean?

Tony: I mean I'm afraid to talk to strangers in strange offices. And they never want to buy from me. I just can't **make good** in this job. I'll never succeed if I don't find another job.

Janet: I'm sure you're exaggerating. You can't be so terrible.

Tony: No, it's true. I always **strike out** when I try to sell my product.

Janet: What do you sell?

Tony: Baby clothes.

Janet: But why do you sell them in offices?

Tony: Because I figured out that people who work in offices probably have children, and those children need clothes.

Janet: You don't **stand a chance** of selling baby clothes in offices. You should go to people's homes to sell them. Show them how nice their children look in them.

Tony: It doesn't matter. I want to **break into** a new profession.

Janet: Which profession?

Tony: I don't know yet. But I think I **have a lot going for** me, and my experience will get me new opportunities. I'm intelligent and a good problem solver. I'm sure I'll **get ahead**. I'll do well in life. I know I'll **get to** use all my talents some day.

Janet: Yeah? Tony, I think you need some help with your job problems.

Tony: Do you have some ideas?

Janet: I have a friend over at the Conway House. She told me they have a job **up for grabs**. They haven't advertised it yet because it only became available yesterday.

Tony: What's the job?

Janet: They need someone to keep track of the mail, remind them of their appointments, and just generally carry out any little jobs they have. You'd be their right-hand man. Interested?

Tony: Wow! It sounds like just what I need. I'd **jump at** a job like that. Should I write them a letter first?

Janet: No, I think you **might as well** go over there directly, since the job hasn't been advertised yet. They could interview you today.

Tony: But I'm not ready yet. What if they ask me questions I can't answer?

Janet: I think, for this kind of job, you'll do better if you don't prepare a lot. Just **play it by ear**. Really, you're perfect. They just want someone who'll do whatever they ask.

Tony: I can do that . . . I hope. Thanks a lot, Janet. If you hadn't told me about this, I would've **missed out on** the perfect job for me. I hope they hire me.

Janet: I have an idea. Since I know some people there, how about if I call them and tell them you're coming? That way, we can make sure you don't **miss the boat**. I'd hate for you to lose this opportunity.

Persuasion

9

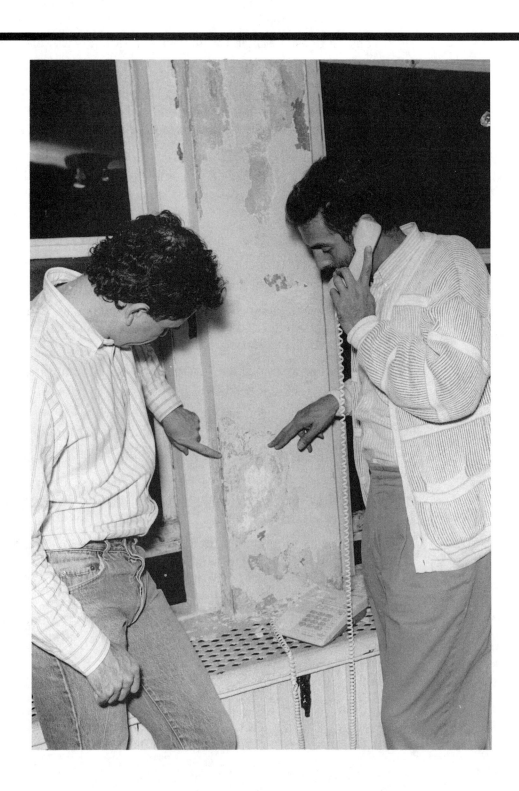

"It's like talking to a brick wall."

Imagine talking to a brick wall! Will it answer you? Can you persuade a brick wall to agree with you? When a person is acting like a brick wall, it's impossible to persuade him. Can you think of a time when you felt like you were talking to a brick wall? What is it about the person's behavior that makes you feel this way? Do you say something like this in your language?

Get Ready

Prepare to hear a conversation by looking at the picture to the left and discussing the questions below with your teacher.

1. What are the two men looking at?
2. Who do you think the one man is calling? Why?

Get the Gist

Answer these questions after you listen to the conversation one time.

A Difficult Landlord

1. What do the speakers want?
2. Why do they think their landlord will refuse?
3. Who is their landlord?

Zero In

Determine the meanings of this chapter's idioms by listening to the conversation again and circling the most likely meaning for each idiom.

1. *talk her into*	argue	persuade	lie
2. *get to the point*	speak directly	arrive	travel quickly
3. *beat around the bush*	work in the garden	speak indirectly	shout
4. *bring up*	suggest	carry	think about
5. *wasting your breath*	getting tired	explaining well	arguing unsuccessfully
6. *get across*	give	explain well	travel

7. *it goes with-out saying*	I disagree	it's ridiculous	it's obvious
8. *talk us out of*	speak angrily to us	refuse to allow us	persuade us not to
9. *get after*	try to persuade	follow	fight with
10. *bring her around*	visit with her	invite her	persuade her
11. *stand up for*	defend	discuss	remember
12. *back down*	return	go away	stop trying to persuade
13. *give in*	stop trying to persuade	be generous	spend money
14. *have the last word*	disagree	say the final argument	pay attention
15. *come around*	visit	start to agree	investigate

Get Your Bearings

Use these exercises to become familiar with the idioms. You may want to refer to the definitions and examples at the end of this chapter while you do them.

Exercise 1: Write T if the statement is true and F if it is false.

_____ *1.* If you want someone to consider your idea, you'll have to bring it up first.

_____ *2.* Only very patient people are likely to say "get to the point."

_____ *3.* When someone agrees with you, the next step is to bring him around.

_____ *4.* We might try to talk a good friend out of moving to another country.

_____ *5.* It's very frustrating when someone else always has to have the last word.

_____ *6.* Good writers are able to get across complicated ideas.

_____ *7.* A doctor should talk a fat patient into eating cakes and candies.

_____ *8.* It goes without saying that people should keep their word.

_____ *9.* To get someone to come around during an argument, we have to give him an invitation.

_____ *10.* We should be proud of someone who stands up for his family.

_____ *11.* If your children aren't learning well in school, you might get after them to study harder.

_____ *12.* A decisive person is one who often backs down.

_____ *13.* Parents who explain homework carefully to their children are wasting their breath.

_____ *14.* A direct person is someone who learned early how to beat around the bush.

_____ *15.* It's easy to solve a disagreement when one party is willing to give in.

Exercise 2: Fill in the blanks in the following dialogue with the idioms listed. Use each idiom only one time.

A.

beat around the bush	come around	bring up
wasting your breath	get after	talk into
it goes without saying	give in	get to the point

Husband: This is a nice old couch, wouldn't you say?

Wife: Yes. I like it very much. It's a wonderful old, traditional piece.

Husband: Yes. Very comfortable too. . . . Of course, it used to be a little more comfortable. You know, before the kids were old enough to bounce on it.

Wife: Are you trying to say something? If you are, please just _____

_____. You're always so indirect! I really dislike it when you

_____ like this.

Husband: Well, now you see why I had to _____ buying a new couch indirectly. I knew you'd be angry if I suggested it directly. I know how you love this old couch.

Wife: Old? This couch is beautiful. It belonged to my parents. I don't want to get rid of it to buy a new one. If you think I will, you're just

_____ .

Husband: Honey, this isn't the first time we've talked about this. How can we bring friends and colleagues home if the house isn't in tip-top shape?*

Wife: I know. You've been _____ me to buy a new couch for a couple of years. It's just that I have so much sentimental value attached to this couch. It was my parents'.

Husband: _____ that the couch is important to you, to both of us. We don't have to get rid of it. Just move it to another room— upstairs perhaps.

Wife: OK. You win, You've _____ me _____ it. Hm. Maybe, since we're buying a new couch, we might as well re-do the whole livingroom. Maybe a different color.

Husband: Wait a minute. This is going to cost us a fortune. I don't think we should buy more than a couch.

* Perfect condition

Wife: Bob, I _____ about getting this couch out of the livingroom. Now it's your turn to _____ on redecorating the livingroom.

B.   **give in**   **have the last word**   **bring around**

        talk out of   **back down**   **come around**

Sam: Tim says he's moving to California.

Fay: Why would he want to do a thing like that? All his friends and family are here.

Sam: Says he's tired of the ice and snow and rain.

Fay: He'll change his mind.

Sam: I don't think so. I've been trying to _____ him _____ it for the past month. But you know him. He always has to _____.

Fay: Maybe Maryann can _____. He always listened to her before.

Sam: I think Maryann is part of the problem. They had a fight last month, and they haven't spoken to each other since then.

Fay: So I guess she won't make him change his mind. Well, maybe he'll _____ on his own. What did he and Maryann fight about?

Sam: I think he wanted to start a new business.

Fay: Another one! He's always talking about starting new businesses. He must have spent a fortune on the last one.

Sam: Yeah. Maryann thinks he's crazy, but he insists on it.

Fay: Well they're both stubborn. Tim has never _____ on any disagreement in his life. He always says he was born to win.

Sam: Yeah, and Maryann's not likely to _____ either. I have to say, I agree with her.

Fay: Yep. California, here Tim comes!*

Exercise 3: You are a children's storybook writer. Your partner, an illustrator, has drawn the illustrations below. Now you have to write captions above them to tell the story of Benny the bunny, who is now old enough to make a life of his own out in the world. Benny has decided to leave his parents and home, but of course they are very worried about him.

* Imitating the song, "California, Here I Come."

Choose idioms from the list below to write captions describing the action in each illustration for your little readers. Some idioms are appropriate for more than one illustration, but use each only one time.

back down	**try to get across**	**get to the point**
talk into	**waste one's breath**	**have the last word**
bring up	✔ **beat around the bush**	**can't talk out of**
	give in	

1. Benny is beating around the bush when he talks to his mother and father.

2. _____

_____

_____

_____

3. _____

_____

_____

_____

4. _____

_____

_____

_____

_____

5. _____

_____

_____

_____

6. _____

_____

_____

_____

7. _____

_____

_____

_____

_____

8. _____

_____

_____

_____

9. _____

_____

_____

_____

10. _____

_____

_____

_____

Tune In

Improve your ability to hear and understand idioms by listening to several news reports and answering the questions below T for True or F for False.

A. Listen to a press conference between the President of the U.S. after his summit meeting with a dignitary from another country and reporters from newspapers and television stations around the country.

_____ *1.* The U.S. president and the other leader reached a new trade agreement.

_____ *2.* The other leader wants trade protection for her country.

_____ *3.* The U.S. President wants the other leader to decrease exports.

_____ *4.* The U.S. President won't say whether he's running for president in the next election.

_____ *5.* The U.S. President is not concerned about the book being published about him.

B. Now listen to the press conference the other leader gave after she arrived back in her country.

_____ *6.* The president of this country said the U.S. government hadn't wanted trade protection until now.

_____ *7.* The U.S. president was able to persuade this president to consider changing her country's trade practices.

_____ 8. The president of this country believes everyone will like the exchange agreement.

_____ 9. It seems that the U.S. President plans to try again to persuade the president of this country to accept a trade protection program.

_____ 10. People in the U.S. are apparently very direct, while people in this president's country are indirect.

Get Down to Business

Improve your ability to use this chapter's idioms in conversation with a couple of your classmates by acting out one or more of the roleplays below.

1. (2 or 3 friends)

You want one or two of your friends to become your roommates and share an apartment instead of living in the dormitory. You figure it will save money on rent and food. They think an apartment costs more than the dormitory and that it requires more responsibility. Convince your friends to share an apartment with you.

Use the following idioms:

bring up	**get to the point**	**get across**
it goes without saying	**come around**	**talk out of**
give in	**talk someone into**	**waste one's breath**
	bring around	

2. (a student and teacher)

You've received a bad grade on a research paper. Try to persuade your teacher to change your grade, or at least to allow you to write it again.

Use the following idioms:

bring up	**beat around the bush**	**get across**
come around	**bring someone around**	**have the last word**
give in		**waste one's breath**

3. (a student and his/her parents)

You've been living in the college dormitory for the past year. It's uncomfortable, expensive, and too noisy to study in. You would like to live in an apartment instead. However, your parents prefer that you stay in the dormitory, where school authorities can keep an eye on you (control your behavior). Discuss the situation and persuade each other of your opinions.

Use the following idioms:

bring up	**beat around the bush**	**get to the point**
talk into	**talk out of**	**get across**

waste one's breath	it goes without saying	get after
have the last word	stand up for	give in
bring around	come around	

4. (2 or 3 college students)

The school vacation is coming soon and you would like to do some traveling around Europe. This would be not only fun, but educational. However, none of you has enough money to do this, so you're going to have to ask your parents for help. You've already asked your parents for money to meet school expenses several times recently, so you have to plan very carefully how to do it this time.

Use the following idioms as you discuss your plan:

bring up	(not) beat around the bush	get to the point
talk into		stand up for
bring around	(not) back down	(not) give in to
	come around	

Put It All Together

Reinforce your ability to speak using many of the idioms you've learned so far by acting out one or more of the roleplays below with your classmates.

1. (a boss and a labor union committee of up to 3)

Your company has been losing money steadily for the past year. Your boss has finally decided that the only way to stop the decrease in profits is to lay off 15–20% of the workers. You believe this is unnecessary and will only make all the workers angry and lead to labor–management problems. Convince your boss not to lay off the workers. (You choose the type of company and product and work out a way to avoid laying off workers.)

Use the following idioms in your discussion:

in time	in the long run	so far
be about to	look forward to	fall behind
pull together	see eye to eye	keep one's word
get out from under	in the red	break even
take something up with	get to the bottom of	back down
	get rid of	take into account
be up to someone	think twice about	(not) stand a chance
might as well	bring up	get after someone
talk out of		

2. (a store manager, 2 parents, a teenaged son or daughter)

Your child has been accused of shoplifting in this department store. You've just arrived to discuss it with the manager, who is very angry and wants to prosecute.

Your child says he or she hadn't intended to take anything, but was running to catch a bus when the security guard stopped him or her and found an expensive watch in his or her coat pocket. The manager recognizes your child from a similar incident 2 months ago. Frankly, you aren't sure that your child *isn't* guilty, but you want to protect him or her anyway. You must convince the manager not to prosecute.

Use the following idioms as you talk:

get across	**waste one's breath**	**back down**
give in	**come around**	**get to the point**
right away	**keep track of**	**keep one's word**
on the spur of the moment	**meet halfway**	**back someone up**
	do without	**be broke**
go through proper channels	**get out of line**	**throw the book at**
give a break	**crack down on**	**be up to someone**

3. (2–3 co-workers and a supervisor)

You are health care workers. All of you believe that you are underpaid. You've examined the salaries of professionals doing comparable work at other hospitals and they earn more than you do. Because your hospital is earning as much profit as these hospitals, you feel this is unfair. Convince your supervisor to raise your salaries.

Use the following idioms in your conversation:

get to the point	**get across**	**waste one's breath**
give in to	**not stand a chance of**	**be up to someone**
take into account	**know the ropes**	**take something up with someone**
make a living by	**make ends meet**	
keep one's word	**put off**	**for the time being**

4. (husband and wife, possibly a teenage child)

You are thinking about buying a car for the first time. You've been married for 18 years and never owned a car, which is very strange in your country. One of you wants a car for the many conveniences it can offer. But the other is more doubtful. Cars can be very inconvenient: the waste of time in repairs and parking, the expense, the maintenance. The teenager wants the car because he or she plans to borrow it all the time. He or she offers to help out with cleaning and maintaining the car.

go without saying	**bring around**	**come around**
give in to	**jump at**	**might as well**
think twice about	**take into account**	**have a voice in**

the ins and outs	**wear out**	**run (cost)**
make ends meet	**take turns**	**keep one's word**
	help out	

Keep the Ball Rolling

Get still more practice with the idioms you've learned so far by participating in a discussion.

Imagine that you are an arbitrator (someone who helps people meet each other halfway) in one or more of the following cases about smoking. What kind of agreement would you try to reach in each?

1. Andy Watson, 58, started smoking when he was just 18 years old. He remembers starting because he wanted to show how "grown up" (adult) it was to smoke. All the advertisements for cigarettes showed tall, muscular, sun-tanned men—often cowboys—smoking cigarettes. Sometimes, they were tall, handsome men in tuxedos with elegant women hanging on their arms. Andy wanted to be like that. Soon, he couldn't have stopped even if he had wanted to. His cigarettes were powerfully addictive—his body craved more and more—until soon he was smoking nearly three packs a day.

   Today, Andy is dying of emphysema and he blames the cigarette companies. He says that they falsely led him to believe that his life would be wonderful if he smoked cigarettes. They didn't tell him that he would become addicted and that he could die from them. He is taking the cigarette company that manufactured his cigarettes to court and suing it for millions of dollars. Some of this money is money he's lost by not being able to work these last 2 years, some is for medical bills, and some is for pain and suffering.

Use the following idioms when you present the results of your discussion:

waste one's breath	**give in to**	**(not) stand a chance**
strike out	**turn down**	**take into account**
scratch the surface	**call for**	**think twice about**
get out from under	**from now on**	**make sense of**

2. Mike Howell, Tina Hart, and Chris Steadwell are taking their company to court because it refuses to prohibit employees from smoking at work. These three employees are allergic to cigarette smoke and, in addition, are aware that, according to researchers, breathing cigarette smoke from other people's cigarettes can cause health problems for them. They asked their company to prohibit smoking at work, but it refused, saying that many employees would be uncomfortable without their cigarettes. Fifty percent of the workers smoke; fifty percent don't. The company claims that it cannot provide smoke-free work environments for some employees because the cost would be very high—architectural changes in the building would be required.

Use the following idioms when you present your results:

crack down on	**take up with**	**go through proper channels**
get across	**stand up for**	
get after	**come around**	**have something going for one**
have a voice in	**out of the question**	
draw the line at	**day in and day out**	**back up**

3. The labor union at National Chemical Company is taking the company to court because the company will prohibit smoking both at work *and* outside of work by next year. The workers believe their privacy is being invaded; they think the company should not be permitted to interfere with their actions at home. The company says the prohibition is necessary because the workers work with a known lung cancer-causing chemical. If they smoke in addition, their chances of serious illness will rise dramatically, and the company will be forced to pay very high health insurance and employee disability bills. The company plans to administer lung-capacity tests occasionally to make sure workers don't smoke. The company will offer smoking-cessation classes for anyone who wants them.

Use the following idioms in your discussion:

go without saying	**stand up for**	**back down from**
might as well	**make a decision about**	**think twice about**
take into account	**gather from**	**crack down on**
do without	**back someone up**	**keep track of**
see eye to eye	**help out**	**for the time being**

Put a Fine Point on Them

Use the following definitions and examples to help you understand the details of this chapter's idioms when you do the exercises.

 1. *bring up*—(S) suggest

> The lecturer brought up a new theory about human development.
> We brought up the idea of a boat party, but nobody accepted it.

 2. *beat around the bush*—make a point very indirectly

> Tommy was afraid to say that he didn't want to go to the horror movie, so he beat around the bush until his mother realized it herself.
> Quit beating around the bush! Tell me what you want.

 3. *get to the point*—speak directly

> I can't figure out what you want when you don't get to the point.
> Our teacher says good writing gets to the point right away.

 4. *talk someone into something*—persuade someone to do something (+ V + ing or + N)

> The president talked his officers into a new agreement after a long meeting.
> Cindy talked her mother into letting her live on the university campus, even though she is very worried about it.

5. *talk someone out of something*—persuade someone not to do something (+ V + ing or + N)

> We talked our teacher out of a lot of homework for the weekend.
> I talked my friend out of moving to Alaska because it's too far away.

6. *get across*—(S) explain successfully

> We had a hard time getting our point across because the reporter interrupted so often.
> Good teachers are able to get across difficult material.

7. *waste one's breath*—explain or argue unsuccessfully

> You're wasting your breath. I won't sell my ring.
> It's too early for the new accountant to ask for a raise. She'll be wasting her breath.

8. *go without saying* (that)—it's obvious (+ noun clause) (subject is usually a noun clause or "it")

> It goes without saying that this election is going to be close.
> That nobody loses weight without controlling food consumption goes without saying.

9. *have the last word*—make the final statement or decision in an argument.

> Peggy always has to have the last word. She's so hard to convince.
> Our manager was very convincing in his explanation, but the director had the last word about the budget.

10. *stand up for*—defend, support

> Joe stood up for tougher anti-smoking laws at the crowded meeting.
> Sue stood up for a friend who was accused of cheating on a test by telling the teacher her friend is always honest.

11. *get after (someone)*—try very hard to persuade someone (often used when the persuasion is considered impolite or too strong)

> Lisa's parents have been getting after her to go to college.
> The lobbyists got after the hospital to lower its charges for poor people.

13. *bring (someone) around*—succeed in persuading; cause to agree

> My mother says 'no.' But don't worry. I'll bring her around.
> My landlady said I can't have a cat, but I think I can bring her around.

13. *back down (from something)*—stop arguing one's position

> The president always refused to raise taxes, but she'll probably back down when her advisors present their evidence for an increase.
> The corporation backed down from its anti-labor statements after the strike ended.

14. *give in (to something or someone)*—stop trying to persuade; agree to do as the opposition wishes (+ V + ing or + N)

> Lisa is giving in to her parents' wishes and enrolling in college.
> I didn't want the meeting to be in my apartment, but I finally gave in to the group. They're coming at 6:00.

15. *come around*—begin to agree

> At first his parents said he couldn't go with his friends on vacation, but they came around later.
> If the manager doesn't come around after the next meeting, we'll have to forget the idea.

Check It Out

Take a closer look at the conversation from the "Zero In" section if you want to see any words or phrases that you might not have understood.

A Difficult Landlord

Rick: Our apartment is starting to look awful.

Dave: Yeah. Needs some paint.

Rick: I don't have money for paint. D'you?

Dave: Nope. Let's ask "the landlady."

Rick: To paint the apartment? We can't **talk her into** that. She's very hard to persuade. You know she never does anything we ask.

Dave: But you're a good talker. Just **get to the point** right away. Be strong and direct.

Rick: I don't think that'll work with her. It'd be better to **beat around the bush** a little. You know, tell her how happy we are here, and remind her that we're good "tenants."

Dave: How will you **bring up** the idea?

Rick: Maybe I'll start by inviting her here to see the place. Then I can bring the painting idea up easily.

Dave: I think you'll be **wasting your breath**. She'll never listen to you.

Rick: That's why I need you to back me up.

Dave: Sure. But how do we **get across** how necessary this is?

Rick: Let's show her the apartment and explain the advantages. I mean, **it goes without saying** that painting improves the value of the apartment. Everyone knows that.

Dave: Good! Of course, she'll still try to **talk us out of** it. She'll say it's too expensive.

Rick: Yeah . . . Well, let's offer to do it ourselves if she buys the paint.

Dave: No. We've been living here for 5 years. This is the first thing we've asked for. I say we **get after** her to paint the place for us. If we plan well, we can **bring her around**. She'll agree in time.

Rick: You're right. We have to **stand up for** our rights. We won't let her change our minds.

Dave: Right! We won't **back down** on this. We'll give her no choice.

Rick: Right! We won't **give in**. We won't change our minds.

Dave: Right! We'll . . .

Rick: You always have to **have the last word**. Can't you let me end a conversation just once?

Dave: Call her.

Rick: Right now?

Dave: Yeah. Call while we're ready. If you do this right, she'll **come around** and then we'll have an apartment that looks like new.

Rick: Yeah. OK. . . . (phone dialing and ringing) Hello, Mom?

Determination

10

"Keep your chin up!"

When you feel like a loser, do you look up or down? How about when you feel like a winner? This expression is used to encourage someone who is losing his determination to succeed. Do you know someone who ought to hear this expression? When do people usually need to hear it?

Get Ready

Prepare to hear a conversation by looking at the picture to the left and discussing the questions below with your teacher.

1. What are the man and woman holding in their arms?
2. What else is the woman holding? What is its use?
3. How do the man and woman spend their time every day?

Get the Gist

Answer these questions after you listen to the conversation one time.

College Dreams

1. Why does the first speaker think college must be hard for Janet?
2. What professions do Ben and Janet want after they graduate?
3. How did Janet become blind?
4. Why is Janet still blind?

Zero In

Determine the meanings of this chapter's idioms by listening to the conversation again and circling the most likely meaning for each idiom.

1. *had my heart set on*	wanted strongly	loved	been afraid
2. *no matter*	not important	absent	wrong
3. *one way or another*	in various styles	easily	certainly

129

4. *makes the most of*	uses to advantage	increases	worries about
5. *make sure*	explain clearly	be certain to	think about
6. *get your way*	get your answer	get knowledge	get your wishes
7. *on purpose*	with previous planning	on the spur of the moment	on time
8. *counted on*	continued	waited	depended on
9. *do it over*	change it	do it again	finish it
10. *once and for all*	definitely	quickly	again and again
11. *go to any length*	travel	try as hard as possible	ask for help
12. *keep on*	continue	prevent	wait
13. *give up*	help others	stop trying	become afraid
14. *took the bull by the horns*	waited and hoped	acted like an animal	acted directly
15. *went for it*	tried to get a goal	traveled	requested something

---

Get Your Bearings

Use these exercises to become familiar with the idioms. You may want to refer to the definitions and examples at the end of this chapter while you do them.

Exercise 1: Read each statement, then determine whether it is T for true or F for false.

_____ *1.* Somebody who plans to get something one way or another might be willing to do something wrong to get it.

_____ *2.* If you have your heart set on something, you ought to see a doctor.

_____ *3.* Doctors like sick patients to give up easily.

_____ *4.* Someone who makes the most of her education is likely to be successful in her life.

_____ *5.* It is not easy to work with someone who must always get his own way.

_____ *6.* You can teach anywhere in the United States, no matter how much English you know.

_____ *7.* Polite children don't keep on talking when someone asks them to be quiet.

_____ *8.* Even though I'm counting on going to college, there's no guarantee that I'll be able to go.

_____ *9.* Children who disobey their parents on purpose should not be punished.

_____ *10.* A good job for someone who likes to take the bull by the horns might be research scientist.

_____ *11.* Someone who will go to any length to win a game might be willing to cheat.

_____ *12.* If I want to apply for a new job and my husband tells me to go for it, he wants me to apply for it.

_____ *13.* When we do things very well, we usually have to do them over.

_____ *14.* We can help make sure we'll be healthy by eating well, exercising, and getting regular physical examinations.

_____ *15.* Sarah said the company refused once and for all to give us another vacation day. This means she has to wait until tomorrow to ask again.

Exercise 2: Choose the best idiom to complete each sentence.

1. I'm so angry. I went to the department store because they had shoes on sale. I _____ buying a certain pair of shoes. But they didn't have them in my size.

 a. made the most of
 b. had my heart set on
 c. went for

2. Georgette is so beautiful. And she really knows how to _____ her eyes by wearing the best colors.

 a. go for
 b. go to any length
 c. make the most of

3. No, I won't forgive you because I know you did it _____.

 a. on purpose
 b. one way or another
 c. once and for all

4. Susan wants to _____ that she'll get the job. She sent a letter to the company after her interview.

 a. count on
 b. go for
 c. make sure

5. He's determined to go to the Far East for his vacation, _____.

 a. on purpose
 b. one way or another
 c. give up

6. My teacher told me that I'm smart enough to _____ a college scholarship.

 a. go for
 b. make sure
 c. give up

7. The weather forecast says we can _____ good weather for the wedding tomorrow.

   a. go to any length
   b. count on
   c. have our hearts set on

8. The president said he would _____ to avoid a war with the other country.

   a. go to any length
   b. go for it
   c. keep on

9. Young children can't drive cars, _____.

   a. on purpose
   b. no matter what
   c. one way or another

10. You won't get what you want unless you ask for it. _____!

    a. Take the bull by the horns
    b. Do it over
    c. Give up

Exercise 3: The Simpsons have had a lot of trouble over the years finding babysitters for their little darling, Horace (better known to previous babysitters as Horace the Little Horror). Tonight, a new babysitter is coming. To prevent the same old problems from happening again, Mr. and Mrs. Simpson have decided to prepare instructions.

Complete their instructions by filling in the blanks with an appropriate idiom from the list below.

has his heart set on	**make sure**	**no matter**
go to any length	**once and for all**	**one way or another**
take the bull by the horns	**get his own way**	**count on**
	make the most of	**given up on**
on purpose	**do them over**	**go for**

How to Keep Our Little Darling Happy

1. Horace's bedtime is 8:00 every night, but he usually _____ staying up until 11 or 12 o'clock. To prevent his getting angry and calling the police, you probably should let him _____. He's usually happiest when he wins.

2. Previous babysitters received occasional physical injuries while watching little Horace. Strangely, they blamed Horace. While it is true that Horace will _____ to get what he wants, we are sure that he would never hurt another person _____. He's simply a high-spir-

ited boy. However, we recommend that you _____ never

to turn your back on Horace, _____ what he tells you. (Like any child, he likes to play little jokes.)

3. We don't like little Horace to have snacks between meals. However, Horace has a large appetite, and he's ingenious about finding ways to get snacks.

Since he's going to eat sweets _____, we have

_____ enforcing this rule. It doesn't make sense to have a rule that a child won't follow, does it?

4. Horace goes to a pre-school for 3-year-olds. Because we want Horace

to _____ his education, we always help him with his homework. Since you will be our substitute for the evening, we'd like Horace

to be able to _____ you for help in the same way that he depends on us. We usually follow this method: We write the answers in his

book and have him _____ on another piece of paper. We believe this method will begin to prepare him for a good career. (We'd like

him to _____ a business degree in college.)

5. We are confident that you can manage little Horace without difficulty. Simply

make sure to _____ when you are with him, as we do.

Children need to know _____ that adults are in control.

Tune In

Improve your ability to hear and understand idioms by listening to several news stories and answering the questions below T for True or F for False.

Radio Sports News

A. Basketball injury

_____ 1. It is surprising that Mooney can play in Saturday's game.

_____ 2. Mooney especially wants to play in the game against Boston.

_____ 3. Dr. Wilson makes it clear that Mooney's progress can be attributed to the medical skill of the hospital.

_____ 4. Mooney will have to have arm surgery again sometime in the future.

_____ 5. Many people believe Tim Ridly wanted to hurt Mooney.

B. Baseball game

_____ 6. In last month's baseball game, Pittsburgh almost lost.

_____ 7. According to the first fan, the Pirates have been playing well.

_____ 8. The second fan thinks San Diego's new players won't help them win this game.

_____ 9. The third fan wants San Diego to win.

_____ 10. The third fan expects San Diego to lose.

C. Baseball team's pitcher

_____ 11. Baseball pitcher Hal Jenkins wants to retire from baseball.

_____ 12. It was Jenkins' idea to return to the team.

_____ 13. It's likely that the team paid Jenkins a lot of money to return to the team.

_____ 14. The team only needs Jenkins for a few weeks.

Get Down to Business

Improve your ability to use this chapter's idioms in conversation with a couple of your classmates by acting out one or more of the roleplays below.

1. (a man and a woman who work together)

You are trying to convince a woman in your office to go out to dinner and the theater (or symphony, or bowling, or a movie) with you this weekend. She insists that she doesn't want to date anyone from the place where she works because it might cause difficulties at work later. She is a career person. You must convince her and promise that nobody at the office will know.

Use the following idioms in your conversation:

no matter	**make sure**	**count on**
one way or another	**on purpose**	**keep on**
get one's way	**give up**	

2. (a woman and a man who work together)

Do roleplay A, but this time, reverse the roles. (The woman asks the man.)

Use the following idioms in your conversation:

make the most of	**have one's heart set on**
go to any length	**go for (something)**
no matter	**take the bull by the horns**
make sure	**one way or another**

3. (an employee and the boss)

You are trying to convince your boss to let you represent your company at a conference in (you pick the place). At the conference, you'll be responsible for giving a presentation about your company's newest product. Your company hopes the conference will lead to many new customers.

Use the following idioms in your discussion:

make the most of	**make sure**	**get one's way**
count on	**go for (something)**	**go to any length**
one way or another	**have one's heart set on**	**take the bull by the horns**

4. (3 people)

You are trying to convince a loved one (someone you care about very much) to stop smoking. The smoker says that he or she has tried to quit many times before but was unable to. You give encouragement and advice.

Use the following idioms in your conservation:

no matter	**one way or another**	**keep on**
give up	**count on**	**do over**
once and for all	**take the bull by the horns**	

Put It All Together

Reinforce your ability to speak using many of the idioms you've learned so far by acting out one or more of the roleplays below with your classmates.

1. (2 parents and a son or daughter)

You want to be a movie star, and the best way to do that is to go to (New York? Paris? London? Hollywood?). Your parents think you will be very disappointed, that you don't know enough about acting to succeed. And they're worried about your living in a big city. However, you are dreaming about fame, fortune, and excitement. Besides, you believe you are very talented. You don't expect to fail. You must try to convince them that you are determined to be an actor in the big city.

Use the following idioms in your discussion:

no matter	**break into**	**make up one's mind**
one way or another	**strike out**	**make ends meet**
make good as	**take the bull by the horns**	**land on one's feet**
go for (something)		**know the ropes**
keep one's word	**go to any length**	**have one's heart set on**
	back somebody up	

2. (an instructor and a small group of students)

You are a driver's education teacher and you are teaching a small class of adults who have failed their driving tests THREE times. Most of them have failed because they got too nervous during the test and made stupid mistakes or argued with the testing officer. Because they have failed so many times, you are devoting tonight's class to building their confidence. Next week, most of them are going to take the test again. They are afraid to take the test next week and expect to fail again.

Use the following idioms in your conversation:

no matter	**one way or another**	**give up**
keep on	**make sure**	**on purpose**
do over	**go for something**	**once and for all**
have what it takes	**get cold feet**	**be about to**
so far	**put off**	**see eye to eye**
talk back	**back out (of)**	**on second thought**

3. (2 drivers)

You've just had a "fender bender" (car accident) at a busy intersection downtown and now you're arguing with each other over whose fault it was. You accuse each other of being terrible drivers who shouldn't be permitted on the road and refuse to back down from your accusations. This is going to be an expensive accident.

on purpose	**once and for all**	**keep on**
waste one's breath	**have the last word**	**back down from**
throw the book at	**from now on**	**(not) have what it takes**
toe the line	**behind schedule**	

4. (a dentist and a patient)

You are a dentist with a patient who doesn't keep his or her teeth in good condition. Your patient doesn't visit your office often enough and doesn't clean teeth carefully enough. As a result, the patient is in danger of losing many teeth before reaching the age of 45. Your patient claims to be too busy to learn about keeping teeth clean and to spend the time necessary to do it every night. Your patient gets home very late from work and wants to eat something and go straight to bed. This patient also loves desserts.

Use the following idioms in your discussion:

one way or the other	**no matter**	**once and for all**
go to any length	**keep on**	**not stand a chance of**
miss out on	**get after**	**the ins and outs**
dawn on	**add up**	

Keep The Ball Rolling

Get still more practice with the idioms you've learned so far by participating in a discussion.

Success—how do we get it? In the U.S., there's a saying, "If at first you don't succeed, try, try again." But is hard work really enough to achieve success? Below is a story* of how one man achieved success. Read it and try to determine what qualities in the man and the situation allowed him to attain this success.

In 1904, the Louisiana Purchase Exposition came to St. Louis, Missouri. This was an ideal opportunity for business people to show their products and increase business. A certain waffle** seller decided the exposition would offer a wonderful opportunity to make a fortune. He took most of the money he had saved and invested it in the ingredients necessary to make waffles as well as syrups to pour over them. During the exposition, people were hungry, so his waffles sold well.

But then disaster struck. He ran out of paper plates. Nobody would want to eat messy waffles without plates and he didn't have enough money to buy more. For hours he visited other vendors and asked to buy plates from them, but nobody wanted to help him; they only had enough for themselves. Finally, he spoke to an ice cream vendor who offered to let the waffle vendor sell ice cream for him. Because it was clear the waffle vendor wouldn't be able to find plates for his waffles, he decided to do the next best thing: earn money by selling ice cream. He agreed and paid the last of his money.

Soon, he was back in his booth, this time selling ice cream. But it worried him terribly that he had spent so much money on waffle ingredients, which he couldn't use now. Suddenly he had a brilliant idea. He went home and cooked some waffles, and, while they were still hot, flattened then until they were very thin, with the help of his wife. Then he rolled them into a cone shape. When they were cool, he put ice cream inside them. Customers flocked to his booth in crowds for the newest desert—an ice cream cone. And by the end of the exposition, the waffle vendor was famous and rich.

Use the idioms below as you state your opinions:

no matter	**one way or another**	**(not) give up**
keep on	**make the most of**	**make sure**
get one's way	**go for something**	**go to any length**
take into account	**give a hand**	**have what it takes**
have something going for one	**miss out on**	**(not) stand a chance**
	get ahead	**get out from under**
it goes without saying	**play by ear**	**come up in the world**

Put a Fine Point on Them

Use the following definitions and examples to help you understand the details of this chapter's idioms when you do the exercises.

1. one way or another/the other—in any way necessary for success
   We'll finish all this work one way or another.
   One way or the other, I'm going to lose weight.

---

* Based on *Seeds of Greatness*, Denis Waitley, p. 193, Pocket Books, 1983.
** A waffle is a flat, fried cake marked with raised squares.

2. *have one's heart set on something*—want very, very much

> The little girl had her heart set on a bicycle, but her mother couldn't afford one.
>
> Sally has her heart set on going to China. I hope she can someday.

3. *give up (on something)*—stop trying (+ V + ing) (compare with *give in*, stop arguing)

> I've given up on studying math. I'll never understand it.
>
> Bill tried to convince us to move to Florida, but he finally gave up when we moved to California.

4. *count on*—depend on

> You can count on me to help you move into your house.
>
> Ben is counting on some videotapes to help him learn French.

5. *get one's (own) way*—get one's wish; win

> Children often get very angry if they don't get their way.
>
> You can't always get your own way. Sometimes you have to meet each other halfway.

6. *go for (something)*—try hard to achieve a much-wanted goal

> Joan isn't sure she's qualified for the new job, but I told her to go for it.
>
> At first I was going to take an apartment near school, but then I decided to go for a house in the suburbs.

7. *make sure*—be determined that something happens (+ "that" clause)

> I'm going to make sure that I get good grades this semester.
>
> Pat made sure that all her co-workers got an invitation to her wedding.

8. *no matter*—it makes no difference; regardless (usually followed by wh- word and clause); frequently used as "no matter what," meaning regardless of anything that happens

> My brother is going to fly home for the holidays no matter what the weather is like.
>
> No matter who you are, you can't borrow a library book without a library card.
>
> I'm going on vacation next week, no matter what!

9. *on purpose*—intentionally; with planning

> Mike tried to tell everyone that he'd made all those spelling mistakes on purpose to test the teacher, but we didn't believe him.
>
> It seemed like the star basketball player missed the basket on purpose. It was such an easy shot.

10. *once and for all*—without doubt; definitely (argumentative, often indicates anger in conversation)

> The president refused, once and for all, to raise taxes.
>
> Once and for all, I want to go to China, not Hawaii.

11. *do over*—(S) repeat an action, often because it was not done well the first time.

> This letter has too many mistakes. You'll have to do it over.
>
> Can I do my composition over? I'm not happy with it.

12. *take the bull by the horns*—attack a difficulty with determination

> You've been worried about your grades for a while. Take the bull by the horns and talk to your teachers about them.

Mr. Jackson took the bull by the horns and demanded to know why the bank refused him a loan.

13. *go to any length*—do anything necessary to achieve something (to + V) (also, *go to great lengths*)

Karen always surprises us. She'll go to any length to get what she wants, even if it hurts other people

A patient must really believe in his doctor; he must know that his doctor will go to any length to keep him healthy.

The TV reporter went to great lengths to interview the family of the victim. First he pretended to be a neighbor, then he offered money.

14. *keep (on)*—continue (+ V + ing)

I'll keep on working until my work is finished.

Sam kept talking even though everyone had fallen asleep long ago.

15. *make the most of something*—use to the greatest advantage

You're a great cook. You know how to make the most of a few ingredients.

Phil made the most of his time with the president to talk about education and social programs.

Check It Out

Take a closer look at the conversation from the "Zero In" section if you want to see any words or phrases that you might not have understood.

Overcoming Adversity

Ben: Janet, isn't it hard for you to take college classes?

Janet: Why? Because I'm blind? Ben, I've **had my heart set on** getting a college degree since I was a young child. My blindness never stopped me from wanting to go to college.

Ben: But it must be hard.

Janet: Sure it is. But I just decided to try **no matter** how hard it was. I always knew that I would go to college **one way or another**. I was absolutely determined to do it. I don't think you'd be any different.

Ben: Maybe not. My whole life I've looked forward to becoming a doctor. It's always been my dream.

Janet: Why did you choose medicine?

Ben: Well, I think it **makes the most of** my abilities. I like to help people, but I also like finding answers to difficult questions. What about you?

Janet: Politics. Oh, I probably can't be a politician. Not until society's attitudes change more. But I'd like to work on someone else's campaign. I just have to **make sure** that I study hard and prepare well.

Ben: I hope you **get your way**. If you don't mind my asking, how did you become blind, Janet? Were you born that way?

Janet: Oh, no. When I was 10, I was hit by a car and hurt my head.

Ben: That's awful. I hope they put the driver in jail.

Janet: No. He didn't do it **on purpose**. It was just an accident.

Ben: Isn't there anything that doctors can do?

Janet: Believe me, they tried. They told me there was an operation that might help. I really **counted on** that, too. I was so sure I wouldn't be blind for long.

Ben: What happened, then?

Janet: The operation didn't work.

Ben: Can't they **do it over**?

Janet: It would be too dangerous to have the operation again. I just had to realize, **once and for all**, that I wouldn't see again. Now I'm used to it.

Ben: I don't think I could have your attitude. Man, I'd **go to any length** to get my vision back, even if it was dangerous. I can't understand why you don't just **keep on** having that operation until it works. I'd have it again and again.

Janet: I used to feel like you. I lost months from my life being so unhappy with my blindness. All I could think about was how to see again.

Ben: But you didn't have the operation again.

Janet: It was impossible. Ben, sometimes you just have to know when to **give up**. I finally realized I was wasting my life trying to get something I couldn't have. So I **took the bull by the horns**. I went to a special school for the blind during the summer.

Ben: Even at only 10 years old, you **went for it**. That's great. I just hope I can work as hard for my goals if anything like this ever happens to me.

Relationships

11

■■■■■■■■■ *"Blood is thicker than water."*

This expression means that family relationships are more important than friendships or working relationships. In the end, people should always depend on or help their family members above all others. Do you agree? Does your language have such an expression? When might you use it?

■■■■■■■

Get Ready

Prepare to hear a conversation by looking at the picture to the left and discussing the questions below with your teacher.

A.

1. Why do you think the woman has a suitcase on the sidewalk?
2. Why is the second woman hugging her?

B.

1. How does the man on the left seem to feel?
2. How is the man on the right reacting?
3. Can you guess what they might be talking about?

■■■■■■■

Get the Gist

Answer these questions after you listen to the conversation one time.

Best Friends

1. What are the two friends talking about?
2. Why is one friend worried?
3. Do you think they are very good friends? Why?

The End of a Friendship?

1. Why are the two friends arguing?
2. Who got the job?
3. Are they still angry with each other by the end of the conversation? How do you know?

Zero In

Determine the meanings of this chapter's idioms by listening to the conversation again and circling the most likely meaning for each idiom.

Best Friends

1. keep in touch with	maintain contact	feel	control
2. give you the cold shoulder	dress warmly	be unfriendly	be generous
3. making new friends	forgetting people	introducing people	starting relationships
4. get along with	be friendly with	travel with	receive
5. get in touch with	shake hands	be friendly	communicate with
6. be cut off from	lose communication	make shorter	remove
7. put up with	accept patiently	believe	give
8. be in the same boat	travel together	live together	have the same problem
9. lose touch with	stop communicating	disagree	forget
10. take care of	throw away	lose	fulfill needs

The End of a Friendship?

11. double-crossed	cheated	blessed	forgotten
12. take you at your word	believe easily	question much	listen carefully
13. get through to	talk to	communicate successfully	hear
14. come between	interrupt	disagree	hurt others' relationship
15. putting me down	releasing me	forgetting me	expressing a bad opinion of me
16. make up	stop fighting	invent	produce
17. be had	be cheated	buy something	steal something

Get Your Bearings

Use these exercises to become familiar with the idioms. You may want to refer to the definitions and examples at the end of this chapter while you do them.

Exercise 1: Read each statement and write T if it is true and F it it is false.

_____ 1. Religious people believe in double-crossing people.

_____ 2. You might cut off someone who lies about you.

_____ 3. People who are shy can make friends easily.

_____ 4. It's difficult to put up with a large, warm, comfortable home.

_____ 5. People who are known to be honest can be easily taken at their word.

_____ 6. If you want to get along with your neighbor, you should give him the cold shoulder in the supermarket.

_____ 7. One way to get in touch with someone is by shaking hands.

_____ 8. Someone who gets along with all kinds of people would make a good salesperson.

_____ 9. If you put down a friend, he'll probably become angry with you.

_____ 10. If you and your classmate are in the same boat, it would be a good idea for you to help each other.

_____ 11. A good nurse shouldn't try hard to take care of the patients.

_____ 12. We should be sure to lose touch with someone who gets bad news.

_____ 13. A couple planning to get married will ask the parents to come between them.

_____ 14. It would be very difficult to get through to someone who didn't speak your language.

_____ 15. If a store advertises a product at a very good price but then doesn't have the product when you try to buy it, you've been had.

_____ 16. After family members argue with each other, they usually want to make up.

Exercise 2: Read the following conversations. Fill in the blanks with the best idioms from the list below.

1. get through to   double-crossed   giving me the cold shoulder

take one at one's word   been had   put up with

Joe: What's wrong with Mary?

Joyce: I don't know. Why do you ask?

Joe: I just said "Hello" to her, and she ignored me. Why do you think she's

_____?

Joyce: Oh. I was talking with her last night and she told me that you

_____ her. She said you're having a party but not inviting her, even though you'd promised her an invitation.

Joe: But that's not true. At first I was going to invite everybody. Then, later, I decided to make it a family-only party. I told her that.

Joyce: So did I, but she feels like she has _____.

Joe: I don't know how to _____ to her. It's so hard to explain things to her because she never believes them.

Joyce: Then she's not a very good friend. A good friend should _____.

Joe: I guess that's true. It's very hard to _____ her not trusting me. I don't want to deal with that anymore.

2. **lose touch with**   **keep in touch**   **get in touch with**

  take care of   **in the same boat**   **put down**

Will: Jeanette, do you know how to _____ Sally? I forgot to ask her a few questions before she left.

Jeanette: She didn't leave a phone number, but she promised to _____ by calling every afternoon. She'll probably call soon, so you can ask her then.

Will: Good. That new customer has a problem, and I don't know how to

_____ it.

Jeanette: I guess we're _____. I need to talk to her about a problem too.

Will: It's a good thing she's only on vacation. If we ever _____ Sally for good, this company will be in big trouble.

3. **make friends**   **put down**   **come between**

  get along with   **cutting him off**   **put up with**

Carol: That's the end. Tim's not my friend anymore. I'm _____.

Linda: Why? What happened?

Carol: We can't _____ each other. He's always so jealous of all my other friends.

Linda: Really? Tim doesn't seem like that kind of person.

Carol: It's true. He can't be friendly with anybody else. Whenever three of us

are talking, he always has to _____ the other person. He criticizes my friends' clothes, the way they talk, and their sports and hobbies.

Linda: It sounds like he's trying to _____ you and your other friends.

Carol: That's right. He wants to be my only friend. It's ridiculous. I can have more than one friend.

Linda: Still, it doesn't seem right to _____ completely.

Carol: I _____ his behavior for a long time, but no more. I

want to _____ without Tim's interference.

Exercise 3: You're an editor at a publishing company. Somehow, some illustrations and their captions were separated. Figure out which title from the list below matches each of the pictures.

Getting in Touch

Getting Along

In the Same Boat

Giving the Cold Shoulder

Making Up

Taking Care of Someone

Double-Crossing

Putting up with It

Making Friends

1. _____

_____

2. _____

_____

3. _____

_____

4. _____

_____

5. _____

_____

6. _____

_____

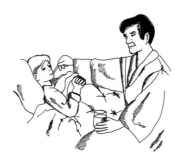

7. _____

8. _____

9. _____

_____

_____

_____

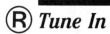

® *Tune In*

Improve your ability to hear and understand idioms by listening to several conversations and answering the questions below T for True or F for False.

A. (a father and son)

_____ 1. The son is nervous about being in the house without his parents.

_____ 2. The father thinks his son and daughter will probably argue a lot.

_____ 3. The father is probably going on a business trip.

_____ 4. The father seems to trust his son.

B. (two friends)

_____ 5. Kathy is as quiet as a mouse in the apartment.

_____ 6. Kathy promised to be quiet before she moved into the apartment.

_____ 7. The woman will probably give Kathy another chance.

_____ 8. The man's sister needs a roommate.

C. (two friends)

_____ 9. The speakers are planning to marry each other.

_____ 10. Janet is too young to get married.

_____ 11. Janet's mother likes her boyfriend, but Janet's father doesn't.

_____ 12. The woman thinks Janet's parents would probably not be happy with any man their daughter might marry.

_____ 13. The man thinks he and Janet will have to live with Janet's parents to make the parents like him.

_____ 14. The woman advises the man to find a way to avoid Janet's parents.

Get Down
to Business

Improve your ability to use this chapter's idioms in conversation with a couple of your classmates by acting out one or more of the roleplays below.

1. (2 sisters or brothers)

You are talking to your sister or brother about a friend who did something that makes you angry. You were planning to ask someone to the school dance next week. You've liked this person for a long time, and you were very nervous about asking him or her. Your friend knew all of this. Without telling you, your friend invited that person to the dance before you could. You are very angry about it. Now you don't have a date for the dance.

Use the following idioms in your conversation:

get along with	**be had**	**be in the same boat**
get through to	**put down**	**get in touch with**
double-cross	**come between**	**give the cold shoulder to**

2. (2–3 friends)

One of your friends has played a joke on you (and another friend) and you're both angry. Your friend told you the test (you choose the subject) was moved up to tomorrow. You've been studying around the clock since you found out. Now your friend tells you that it was all a joke. This friend is always playing jokes on you and others. You want the friend to stop it once and for all or lose your friendship.

Use the following idioms in your conversation with this friend:

double-cross	**be had**	**cut off**
take someone at his word	**be in the same boat**	**put up with**
	get through to	**get along with**
cut off	**give the cold shoulder to**	**put down**
make up		**come between**

3. (2–3 friends)

Some friends of yours are moving to another country because of the husband's or wife's job. You may never see them again and you're going to miss them terribly. You've driven them to the airport and now you're saying goodbye.

keep in touch	**(not) lose touch**	**take care of**
make friends	**(not) come between**	**(not) cut off**
get along with	**get in touch**	**take (one) at his or her word**

4. (2 friends, by telephone)

When you were in college, you had a very good friend with whom you did everything. You had similar interests, similar talents, and similar outlooks on life.

After graduation, you were separated by jobs and marriage. Recently you've been thinking a lot about this friend and have decided to telephone him/her. In the beginning of this conversation, you are trying to figure out why you lost touch completely.

Use the following idioms in your conversation:

keep in touch with	**get in touch with**	**lose touch with**
get along with	**come between**	**be cut off from**
go for something	**make friends with**	

Put It All Together

Reinforce your ability to speak using many of the idioms you've learned so far by acting out one or more of the roleplays below with your classmates.

1. (3–4 friends)

You've been very good friends for a long time (you decide how long). One of your husbands or wives has been offered a job on the other side of the country and you don't think that you want to go. Your friends are helping you to see that living in the other place might not be as bad as you think, but you disagree. You'd prefer to convince your husband or wife not to accept the other job so that you can stay with your friends and family.

turn down	**make up one's mind**	**get cold feet**
play by ear	**out of the question**	**make the most of**
get ahead	**do without**	**hand in hand**
(be) cut off from	**get through to**	**make friends**
come between	**waste one's breath**	**lose touch**
back someone up	**come through for**	**look forward to**

2. (husband and wife)

Your mother- and father-in-law (you decide whose parents) have just gone home to their city and you are really glad. It was a tough weekend visit. Your in-laws don't like you very much because they think you don't work hard enough for your family. Your in-laws sometimes said unkind things about you to your spouse over the weekend. Now you are discussing the weekend with your spouse and how to communicate with your in-laws in the future.

Use the following idioms in your conversation:

keep in touch with	**(not) get along with**	**(not) be cut off from**
give the cold shoulder to	**put up with**	**make up**
	make friends with	**come between**
put down	**waste one's breath**	**bring around**
scratch the surface	**have the last word**	

3. (a student and teacher)

You developed a nice relationship with a student while he/she was in your school. Now the student is graduating, looking for a job in the business field. You would like to help the student with his/her career in the future. Today you are saying goodbye and offering advice on how to be successful.

Use the following idioms in your conversation:

keep in touch	**take care of**	**make sure**
make good as	**get ahead**	**get cold feet**
play by ear	**help out**	**do a favor**
get one's own way	**keep on**	**make the most of**

4. (3–4 co-workers)

You've heard that your company is going to lay off some employees because its profits are low this year. Because you are the newest employees, you're pretty sure you are among those who'll be laid off. As additional evidence, your boss hasn't been very friendly to you recently. You and your co-workers are discussing the problem, your future plans, and possible ways to fight the lay-off.

Use the following idioms in your discussion:

give the cold shoulder to	**keep in touch**	**be in the same boat**
	give in to	**have the last word**
strike out	**stand up for**	**get cold feet**
no matter	**count on**	**not stand a chance of**
make the most of	**take the bull by the horns**	**might as well**
talk someone out of something		**take someone at his word**

Keep the
Ball Rolling   Get still more practice with the idioms you've learned so far by participating in a discussion.

You are family counselors whose job is to help people solve family problems. Read about one or both of the problems below and discuss with each other what should be done about them.

1. Anna Smith is 67 years old. Three months ago, she had a mild stroke (cerebral hemorrhage) which left her right side slightly weak. She is able to speak only with difficulty. Anna has two children, a married son who is 45 and lives 700 miles from Anna and a married daughter who is 40 and lives 1200 miles from Anna. They each have two teenaged children and work full time. They earn middle incomes. Each has asked Anna to come live with them, but Anna has refused. She has valued her independence very highly since her husband died 5 years ago, and she always promised herself that she would never interfere with her children's lives. Since Anna refuses to live with them, her children are trying to convince her to live in a nursing home. But she sees no reason why she shouldn't continue to live alone.

Where should Anna live? Should she be forced to live with one of her children? Should she be forced to live in a nursing home? What can be done to ensure her safety and happiness?

Use the following idioms as you give the results of your discussion:

keep in touch with	**get in touch with**	**lose touch with**
cut off	**it goes without saying**	**take care of**
put up with	**in time**	**make friends**
give up	**miss out on**	**might as well**
have a voice in	**give a hand**	**help someone out**
come through for	**make ends meet**	**do without**
make sure	**one way or the other**	**bring someone around**

2. The Corelli family has come to see you about their son, Ronnie, who is now 7 years old. Ronnie has been going to a public school for a year and a half. While Ronnie was home all day, when he was younger, his parents were able to make excuses for his unusual behavior. But now that he's with other children his age, it has become clear that his intelligence level is significantly lower than average. His school has asked the Corelli's to remove him because it doesn't have the facilities or personnel to teach retarded children well. The principal of the school is recommending a government funded institution 50 miles outside of the Corelli's town. Ronnie will have to live there and come home only on weekends. Because it's a government school, the Corelli's will not have to pay tuition. However, they don't want to send Ronnie so far from home, where he might not get the same loving care he receives with his family. They believe Ronnie needs personal attention in order to learn. The Corelli's have two other children, ages 5 and 9.

Is it reasonable for the neighborhood school to refuse to accept Ronnie? How would education at the government school compare to education at the neighborhood school? Should Ronnie be forced to go to the government school? Should the Corelli's hire a lawyer and try to force their neighborhood school to accept Ronnie? Should they keep Ronnie at home and educate him themselves?

Use the following idioms as you explain your decisions:

cut off	**take care of**	**put up with**
one way or the other	**no matter**	**bring around**
get ahead	**take something up with**	**count on**
miss out on	**make friends with**	**make sure**
draw the line at	**get rid of**	**it goes without saying**
stand up for	**be up to someone**	

Put a Fine Point on Them

Use the following definitions and examples to help you understand the details of this chapter's idioms when you do the exercises.

1. *keep in touch (with someone)*—maintain contact or communication
   I still keep in touch with my childhood friends by writing long letters.
   Keep in touch while you're in Florida. They have post offices and telephones there too!

2. *get in touch (with someone)*—communicate with; contact
   When she discovered she'd been robbed, Mary got in touch with her parents.
   I was in my hometown for a few days, so I got in touch with all my old friends.

3. *lose touch (with someone)*—lose contact or communication, not on purpose
   After graduation, all of us moved to different cities and lost touch.
   Andy lost touch with his friends when he went into the army.

4. *get along (with someone)*—have a good relationship; be friendly
   Everyone thinks he's a good manager because he gets along with all the employees in his department.
   All the neighbors in Greta's neighborhood get along. They're a friendly group.

5. *double-cross (someone)*—betray; break a trust
   The new product designer double-crossed his company. He gave some of his best designs to another company.
   My boss double-crossed me by promising me a promotion but giving it to someone else.

6. *be had*—be cheated
   The advertisement promised a beautiful diamond ring for $19.95 so I bought it. But I was had. When it arrived it was only cheap glass.
   We were had. Tony said this apartment would be lovely, but it's awful.

7. *cut off*—(S) stop communication; end a relationship

Mr. Chang is so angry about his son's behavior that he has cut him off. He refuses all his son's phone calls.

Shirley cut off her brother after he tried to sell her car without permission.

8. *give the cold shoulder (to someone)*—(S) be unfriendly; refuse to speak to someone

Sue gave me the cold shoulder at the party. She's still angry about our argument.

Tom gave the cold shoulder to his roommate, who always plays the stereo too loudly.

9. *be in the same boat*—have the same problem

My roommate and I are in the same boat. Neither of us can find a new apartment to live in during the summer.

Both the western and the eastern parts of the country are experiencing a drought. We're all in the same boat.

10. *take someone at his word*—believe what someone says without having evidence. (This phrase often actually indicates disbelief, but since no evidence is available, the listener feels he must agree to believe.)

The police officer wouldn't take me at my word when I told her I was driving fast because I needed to get to the hospital. She accompanied us the whole way.

The mother took her little boy at his word when he said he hadn't eaten any cookies. She didn't check the cookie jar or his mouth.

When the student said she couldn't give the teacher her research paper because she'd been sick, the teacher answered doubtfully, "I'll take you at your word."

11. *take care of*—fill someone's needs

A babysitter takes care of children while their parents are away from home.
Would you please take care of this customer?

12. *get through to someone*—communicate successfully

I wasn't sure I'd be able to get through to my cousin from Mexico because I don't speak much Spanish, and she doesn't speak any English.

Adults sometimes have trouble getting through to children.

13. *put up with someone/something*—accept a difficulty patiently; tolerate

Bobby's so noisy. I have trouble putting up with his crying.

How can you put up with Pat? She's always bragging.*

14. *put down someone*—(S) show a lack of admiration or respect for someone, insult

It's obvious the director has little respect for her assistant. She often puts him down in public.

The Congressman put down the TV reporters for ignoring the important issues in their newspaper stories.

15. *make friends with someone*—establish a friendship

People usually make friends with those who have similar personalities and interests.

I'd like to make friends with him, but I never have an opportunity to do it.

---

* Speaking about herself in admiration.

16. come between (two people)—cause difficulty in others' relationship

> Ted was jealous of his friend's relationship with Ted's old girlfriend and tried to come between them.
>
> My father-in-law has been coming between my wife and me by saying unkinds things about me to her. I think he wants her to divorce me.

17. make up with (someone)—reestablish a good relationship after being angry

> Sometimes I think that Tom and Cathy like to fight because they enjoy making up so much.
>
> My best friend made me so angry last week that I refused to make up with her. She isn't a good friend.

Check It Out

Take a closer look at the conversation from the "Zero In" section if you want to see any words or phrases that you might not have understood.

Best Friends

Mary: You must be excited to be starting a new life.

Debbie: Yeah, but nervous too. A completely new city is a big change in my life.

Mary: I'm sure you'll like San Francisco. I hope you plan to **keep in touch with** all of us.

Debbie: Sure. I'll write and telephone as often as I can. I'm not planning to **give you the cold shoulder** after I get married. I'll still communicate with all of you.

Mary: We're counting on it.

Debbie: Actually, I'm a little worried about **making new friends** in San Francisco. It's such a big city. I might be lonely there.

Mary: No, I'm sure you won't have any trouble meeting people and making friends. You **get along with** people very well. You're a very friendly person. You shouldn't worry so much.

Debbie: I hope you're right. By the way, I forgot to give you my new address.

Mary: That's right. I need to know how to **get in touch with** you after you move. The last thing I want is to **be cut off from** my best friend. I'll need your letters and phone calls.

Debbie: (laughing) I feel sorry for myself. Nobody else will **put up with** my bad jokes. You're the only one who ever laughs at my jokes.

Mary: My jokes have always been terrible too. As joke tellers, we're **in the same boat**, I'm afraid. We both tell terrible jokes.

Debbie: Promise me that we won't **lose touch with** each other, bad jokes included.

Mary: I promise to write and call often. And I promise to **take good care of** your cat, too.

The End of a Friendship?

Jim: We're finished. I don't ever want to talk to you again.

Bob: What did I do?

Jim: You **double-crossed** me, that's what. I told you I was going to apply for that computer programming job, and you applied before me.

Bob: I didn't think you were sure about applying. You always say things you don't mean. I didn't **take you at your word** this time.

Jim: I just can't **get through to** you. How can I make you understand that I wanted that job?

Bob: Your mother told me that you didn't really want it.

Jim: That's crazy. She would never say that. She knows that's not true. You're just trying to cause trouble. You're trying to **come between** my mother and me.

Bob: You're the one who's crazy. You've never been able to control your anger.

Jim: Now you're attacking me. I can't believe you're **putting me down** like this. It's so insulting.

Bob: Look. It doesn't matter. We might as well **make up** because neither of us got the job. So we can just stop arguing.

Jim: What?

Bob: The new assistant got it.

Jim: But he has no experience. That's not fair.

Bob: I know that. We've **been had**. That job shouldn't have gone to him. The company cheated us again.

Jim: Well, we have to fight this.

Bob: How?

Jim: Let's sit down and make a plan to . . .

Competition

12

"You win some, you lose some,"

This expression means, "OK, today I lost. But I'll win again some other day." It's used to admit defeat without showing any anger or sadness. Would you use this expression after you lost your job or failed your college entrance examination? When might you use it?

Get Ready

Prepare to hear a conversation by looking at the picture to the left and discussing the questions below with your teacher.

1. What are the man and woman reading in the newspaper?
2. Do they look happy about the news? Can you guess why?

Get the Gist

Answer these questions after you listen to the conversation one time.

Election Surprise

1. What are the two speakers talking about?
2. Why did the candidate quit the election?
3. How do the speakers feel about her quitting the race?
4. Why will the speakers' second-choice candidate have trouble winning the election?

Zero In

Determine the meaning of this chapter's idioms by listening to the conversation again and circling the most likely meaning for each idiom.

1. *out of the running*	out of the contest	very tired	away from exercise
2. *out of his way*	lost	unable to stop him	confused
3. *get the better of*	defeat	understand	talk to

4. catch up to	find	hold	do as well as
5. go head to head with	exchange ideas	hit	compete directly
6. got a jump on	became afraid	got an advantage	exercised
7. cream of the crop	wealthy	the best of all	delicate
8. was up against	disliked	competed against	succeeded with
9. fair and square	without cheating	old-fashioned	unhappy
10. get even with	count carefully	be the same	get revenge
11. get back at	get revenge	return	walk behind
12. face to face	in the presence of	strongly	with difficulty
13. keep her from	hold	prevent	continue
14. showing off	displaying oneself	stopping	remembering proudly
15. has two strikes against	is unemployed	has some disadvantages	wins
16. keeping up with	controlling	continuing	going at the same speed

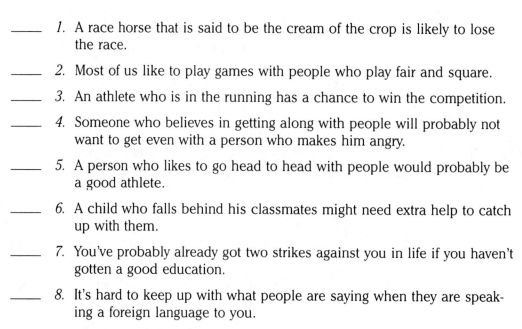

Get Your Bearings

Use these exercises to become familiar with the idioms. You may want to refer to the definitions and examples at the end of this chapter while you do them.

Exercise 1: Read the following statements and mark them T for true or F for false.

_____ 1. A race horse that is said to be the cream of the crop is likely to lose the race.

_____ 2. Most of us like to play games with people who play fair and square.

_____ 3. An athlete who is in the running has a chance to win the competition.

_____ 4. Someone who believes in getting along with people will probably not want to get even with a person who makes him angry.

_____ 5. A person who likes to go head to head with people would probably be a good athlete.

_____ 6. A child who falls behind his classmates might need extra help to catch up with them.

_____ 7. You've probably already got two strikes against you in life if you haven't gotten a good education.

_____ 8. It's hard to keep up with what people are saying when they are speaking a foreign language to you.

_____ 9. It's very pleasant to be around people who show off a lot because they are so friendly.

_____ 10. Job interviewers like to meet applicants face to face.

_____ 11. When you miss someone a lot, you want to get back at him quickly.

_____ 12. It's pleasant to be around people who always try to get the better of us.

_____ 13. It's easier to win a competition when nobody is in your way.

_____ 14. You should be grateful when a friend or family member tries to keep you from making a terrible mistake.

_____ 15. It's harder to win when you are up against tough competition.

_____ 16. It's wrong to get a jump on our work.

Exercise 2: Fill in the blanks with the correct idiom from the list. Use each idiom one time. Some may be appropriate in more than one blank.

Sports Talk

fair and square	**catching up to**	**get back at**
going up against	**keep up with**	**face to face**

Al: Boy! That was a great game yesterday, wasn't it?

Charlie: Sure was. I can't believe how hard the Spitfires played. I never expected them to win.

Al: I did. They've been lousy* all season. They had to start

_____ the other teams soon or they wouldn't stand a chance of winning the championship.

Charlie: Yeah. Besides, the Tornados got so many points the last time, I guess the

Spitfires just wanted to _____ them this time.

Al: You going to the next game?

Charlie: Against the Bulldogs? No way! They never play _____.
Man, they cheat all the time. Anyway, they're too good for the Spitfires.

There's no way the Spitfires could _____ the Bull-dogs.

Al: I know all that. I'd just like to see old Mad-Dog Johnson in action again.

Can you imagine our team _____ with Mad-Dog?

Charlie: That *could* be pretty good. I don't know. Maybe I'll go. I wouldn't mind

seeing Mad-Dog _____ instead of just on TV.

* Slang for "awful."

Slow in School

go head to head	**face to face**	**go up against**
showing off	**have two strikes against**	**get the better of**
get even with	**fair and square**	

Teacher: Hello, Mrs. Timmons. How have you been?

Mrs. Timmons: Fine. But I'm a little worried about Jimmy. He doesn't seem to be very happy lately.

Teacher: I've been noticing that, and I was planning to call you soon. I think he's been having a little trouble with his classmates.

He's been _____ a little lately by bringing some of his more expensive toys into the classroom. Some of the other students are jealous.

Mrs. Timmons: Really? I don't know how he could manage that without my knowing about it. I'm very surprised.

Teacher: Well, I think the problem is deeper than that. He also has been cheating at some of the games we play. He doesn't seem to want

to play _____ anymore and the other children are angry because they play by the rules. They don't want to

_____ him in any games now because they know they won't be able to win.

Mrs. Timmons: What happened yesterday? He came home with a small hole in his pants. I asked him about it, but he didn't want to tell me.

Teacher: There was a small fight during lunch. Some of the bigger kids

decided to _____ him for cheating. They wanted to get a little revenge. Oh, you don't have to worry. Jimmy is a tough little boy. He'll _____

_____ anybody who threatens him. He's a winner. Nobody

can _____ Jimmy.

Mrs. Timmons: Well I certainly don't want him fighting in school. It's not proper behavior and, besides, he _____. He's much smaller than the other children. I'll talk to him tonight, and would you please let me know if this behavior continues?

Teacher: Of course. I can telephone you or, if you prefer to talk

_____, we can meet again.

Exercise 3: Today is your first day on the job as a sports writer for a large daily newspaper. But you feel terrible because you just handed in a story to the sports editor and he gave it back with the word BORING! at the top.

Looking it over, you realize your language was rather dull for a sports story. Cross out the phrases your editor underlined, and add more exciting language from the list of idioms below.

fair and square	**get the better of**	**face to face**
get even with	**in the running**	**go head to head with**
in his way	**cream of the crop**	**keep them from**
showing off	**go up against it**	**keeping up with**
	have two strikes against it	

Flames Compete with Wolves Sunday

The <u>best athletes</u> in football will <u>compete against</u> each other this Sunday when

the Flames and the Wolves meet <u>each other directly for</u> the Super Bowl. And it promises to be one of the most <u>exciting games in years</u>, given the teams' histories.

Flames manager Ray Hughes admits that his team <u>has some disadvantages</u> with

star player Michael Joyner injured. But he says that won't <u>stop them from</u> winning their second Super Bowl ring.

"We have plenty of fine players on the team. I'm not worried about that." With

or without Joyner, Hughes said fans can be sure the Flames will be <u>in the contest</u>. "What worries me more is the Wolves' attitude," said Hughes.

Even some of his teammates admit that Marks was having trouble <u>maintaining</u>

<u>the same speed as</u> Joyner during most of the game. They say, unofficially, that he

may have tried to <u>defeat</u> Joyner early in the game by hurting him.

Marks denies this, admitting only that he may have been guilty of <u>attracting</u>

<u>attention to himself</u>, but not of deliberately hurting another player. "If he says I did that, he's wrong," said Marks. "The only important thing in football is getting

the ball into the end zone." Marks said he might hurt any player who <u>hindered his</u>

<u>success</u> during a football play, not just the other team's star player.

For fans, the question now is whether the Flames will try to <u>get revenge against</u> the Wolves in Sunday's game. But there's no question it'll be an exciting game.

Tune In

Improve your ability to hear and understand idioms by listening to several conversations and answering the questions below T for True or F for False.

A. (a man and woman)

_____ 1. The woman thinks the man is a poor athlete.

_____ 2. The man's wife is a better runner than he is.

_____ 3. The man used to think his wife was not in good physical shape.

_____ 4. The man thinks his wife cheated.

_____ 5. The man wants to participate in another race only if his wife does too.

B. (high school boy and girl)

_____ 6. The girl was surprised that one of the schools didn't accept her.

_____ 7. The school that rejected her was not a very good school anyway.

_____ 8. The boy has applied to several schools but doesn't expect to be accepted.

_____ 9. The boy wasn't a very good student in high school.

_____ 10. The boy has decided not to give up on going to college.

C. (grandmother and granddaughter)

_____ 11. The grandmother thinks beauty contests can help young women become businesswomen.

_____ 12. The granddaughter enjoyed watching the Miss Apple Tree contest, but she dislikes such contests in general.

_____ 13. The grandmother is encouraging Susan to take part in the next Miss Apple Tree contest.

_____ 14. The Miss Apple Tree contest gives the winner money for college.

_____ 15. The grandmother was hoping a different woman would win the contest.

Get Down to Business

Improve your ability to use this chapter's idioms in conversation with a couple of your classmates by acting out one or more of the roleplays below.

1. (1 or 2 parents and a 12-year-old child)

Your child has just come home and is very upset about losing a contest at school (you decide what kind of contest). The child wants to blame the loss on the other children or the teacher by saying that the contest wasn't fair in some way. You know that your child cannot always win and you believe that's an important lesson to learn. It's especially important that your child learn that lesson now because your child is planning how to get revenge on his or her classmates and the teacher.

Use the following idioms in your conversation:

fair and square	**catch up to**	**go head to head**
cream of the crop	**be up against**	**get even with**
get back at	**keep one from**	**show off**
keep up with	**have two strikes against**	**make up**

2. (2 or 3 friends)

There's a big sports game on television tonight (you choose the sport). You and your friends are planning to watch it together. You're already at one friend's house and the game starts in about 20 minutes. One of the teams is considered to be the best in the sport this year and has a great record. The other has a lot of young players who are inexperienced but very talented. Its record is pretty poor. You're arguing about which team will win this game and whether either team will win the championship. This argument is also a matter of pride, because each of you considers himself or herself to be an expert on this sport.

Use the following idioms in your discussion:

out of the running	**in the running**	**get the better of**
cream of the crop	**catch up to**	**go head to head**
be up against	**have two strikes against**	
keep up with	**keep one from**	

3. (a teacher and a student)

Your teacher is accusing you of cheating on an entrance examination to a special program in your school. This program can give you a real advantage when you apply to college (or graduate school). Yet only a small number of people in your school will be chosen, so the examination is very competitive. Your teacher saw you looking at the paper of the person next to you. You honestly didn't mean to cheat. You are not a dishonest person. Yet without thinking, you actually did look at that person's paper, though you did not use anything that you saw. You need to convince your teacher that you are honest and that you didn't copy anything that you saw.

Use the following idioms:

in the running	**out of the running**	**be up against**
fair and square	**face to face**	**keep one from**
cream of the crop	**have two strikes against**	**go head to head**

4. (2 teachers)

Your high school will be giving an examination to its students for entrance into the accelerated learning program—a special group of classes that prepares students especially well for university majors in the health fields.

You have one student in particular who you know is interested in a health career and who is extremely intelligent. You'd like to see this student do well on the examination. However, the student's parents prefer him or her to work in the family business, a small store. Even now, the student has little time to study because he or she has to work so often in the store. In addition, only the top 10% of all students will be accepted in the program. Most other students are receiving special tutoring to prepare. Your student cannot afford such tutoring. You are discussing what to do about this student.

Use the following idioms in your discussion:

be out of/in the running	**go head to head with**	**catch up with**
cream of the crop	**keep someone from**	**be up against**
have two strikes against	**fair and square**	**get a jump on**

Put It All Together

Reinforce your ability to speak using many of the idioms you've learned so far by acting out one or more of the roleplays below with your classmates.

1. (a political candidate and 2 or 3 newspaper/television reporters)

New telephone surveys, 2 weeks before the election, indicate that voters are picking you second out of seven candidates for (you decide the political office). Reporters are now asking your opinion about the surveys, the number 1 candidate, your chances for winning, and your finances. You are especially interested in having a televised debate with your opponent. You believe the only survey that really counts is the election itself.

Use the following idioms in this "press conference":

get the better of	**face to face**	**catch up to**
keep up with	**jump at**	**make up one's mind**
come around	**get across**	**one way or the other**
land of one's feet	**call for**	**ahead of time**
for the time being	**be about to**	**fall behind**
in the red	**go broke**	**break even**
get a jump on	**just around the corner**	

2. (3–4 company executives)

You've been working on developing a new car for the past 2 years: It looks like a spaceship, has very low fuel consumption, and costs less than most cars its size. Now you discover that another company has developed virtually the same car and is planning to put it on the market next month. You believe that company had an industrial spy steal the plans for your car, and you're very angry. You're trying to figure out how it happened and what to do about it.

Use the following idioms in your discussion:

get the better of	**get even with**	**keep someone from**
be up against	**show off**	**fair and square**
get after	**(not) give in to**	**make sure**
take the bull by the horns	**(not) put up with**	**double-cross**
	no matter	**add up**
be had	**keep track of**	**fall behind**
dawn on	**crack down on**	**get a jump on**
throw the book at		

3. (3 or 4 students in the police academy) (or soldiers in the army)

You are the top three cadets (students) in the police (army) academy. You have heard that only one cadet of the top three will be chosen for a position in the police force (or for a promotion in the army) at the end of the training course, in 1 month. The three of you have been very good friends all during your training and this competition is sure to put a strain on your friendship. You discuss the problem with each other, trying to find a way to save your friendship as one of you advances in his or her career.

Use the following idioms:

go head to head with	**go up against**	**fair and square**
keep one from	**get along with**	**be in the same boat**
come between	**miss the boat**	**think twice about**
back out of	**keep on**	**one way or the other**
(not) stand a chance	**get ahead**	**have what it takes**
strike out	**no matter**	

4. (a committee—up to 4 persons)

Your committee has been given the job of finding the perfect person to fill a new job in the company (you choose the job title and the business). You have just finished interviewing the top three candidates, and it's now time to make a decision.

The first candidate has had an excellent education and a lot of experience. However, this candidate may not be aggressive enough to deal with the people who work in your company. In your business, people have to be tough.

The second candidate is very personable (friendly) and seems to be aggressive enough. But even though this candidate has the appropriate education, his or her experience in the field is limited.

The final candiate has the right experience and education, is even aggressive enough, but his or her personality is very strong and his or her appearance doesn't quite match the company's requirements.

It's clear that these are the three best people you'll find. Now you need to pick one of them.

Use the following idioms in your discussion:

out of the running	**in the running**	**go head to head**
cream of the crop	**go up against**	**face to face**
have two strikes against	**keep up with**	**get the better of**
	gather from	**think twice about**
out of the question	**take into account**	**have what it takes**
might as well	**give someone a break**	**the ins and outs**
know the ropes		

Keep the Ball Rolling

Get still more practice with the idioms you've learned so far by participating in a discussion.

Sports Violence

Violence during sports events such as soccer, football, and basketball has been increasing in recent years—enough so that people have discussed trying to control it. Read the following story about an example of sports violence, then work with your committee on the problem below.

The Lions were losing the game, 109 to 107 with only 12 seconds left. All their best players were tired, so the coach did the only thing he could. He gestured for Stevens to come over. The crowd knew what to expect. Stevens was a lousy basketball player, but there was one thing he could do well . . . very well indeed. Stevens was the bruiser, the guy with the million dollar fist. When Stevens came into a game, the game wasn't basketball anymore but boxing.

"Get in there and knock out Johnson," the coach said. "We need time to shoot. Don't let the other team get in there." And Stevens ran onto the court to do the thing he does best, hurt someone.

When the referee wasn't looking, Stevens slammed his elbow into the face of the other team's best player, Johnson. Johnson was hurt so badly that he had to leave the game. Without his skill, his team lost. Johnson suffered a broken jaw and won't be able to return to the basketball court for 2 months.

If Stevens had done this out on the street, he would have been arrested and possibly jailed for assault. But he did it during a sporting event—no arrest, no punishment.

You and the members of your group are on a committee created to formulate rules for all basketball teams governing violence such as that described above. In formulating these rules, you'll need to consider the following points:

- what types of acts constitute "unnecessary" violence
- whether or not rules are actually a good idea
  —what the causes of sports violence are
  —how effective rules will be in limiting violence
  —what effects rules might have on the game itself
- if they are necessary, what the rules should be
  —when an athlete should be punished
  —whether there should be different levels of punishment
  —how strict the strongest punishment should be

Use the following idioms as you present your decisions and reasons to your classmates. You may want to share the presentation: for example, one student to explain the history of the problem, one to explain the causes of the problem, one to explain the rules.

go to any length	**get the better of**	**crack down on**
fair and square	**once and for all**	**on purpose**
get even with	**get back at**	**keep someone from**
get after someone	**one way or the other**	**throw the book at**
get rid of	**draw the line at**	**think twice about**
(not) stand a chance	**make sure**	**take into account**
put an end to	**call for**	**by all means**
take the bull by the horns		

Put a Fine Point on Them

Use the following definitions and examples to help you understand the details of this chapter's idioms when you do the exercises.

1. *get the better of (someone)*—defeat, get an advantage over

   My roommate got the better of me in the card game.
   Paul tries to get the better of everyone. That's why nobody likes him much.

2. *face to face*—in the presence of; in person

   I could have sent a letter, but I decided to get in touch with her face to face.
   When you can't talk face to face with someone, the telephone is a good substitute.

3. *get even (with someone)*—get revenge (compare to *get back at*)

   Sam was so angry with his noisy neighbors that he decided to get even with them. He's going to have a party every Saturday this year.
   After the company took away the employees' health benefits, the employees got even by going on strike.

4. *be out of the running*—have no chance to achieve something

Tim applied for the opening in the systems analysis department, but he's already been told he's out of the running. They're considering giving the job to one of three other applicants.

Because Mary's out of the running for president of her class, she's going to try to become vice president.

be in the running—have a good chance to achieve something

I don't know if Tom's going to get the house he wants to buy, but he's certainly in the running if you consider the amount of money he offered.

Ms. Holt says she doesn't know whether I'll get the job, but she thinks I'm definitely in the running.

5. *go head to head with (someone over something)*—compete with directly, strongly

I'm not surprised that Ann wasn't chosen to represent the company at the conference. She goes head to head with anyone who disagrees with her. We need someone who's more subtle.

The government's lawyer went head to head with the defendant's lawyer over the date of the trial. The defendant's lawyer wanted to put it off.

6. *out of one's way*—unable to stop one; out of competition (also, out of *the* way)

Terry thinks she can get the job now that her chief rival is out of her way.

With the other team out of the way, our team should be able to win.

in one's way—able to stop one; being a hindrance or problem (also, in *the* way)

Fred wanted a promotion, but his lack of college education stood in his way.

Every time I want to talk to the director, her secretary gets in my way.

7. *catch up (with* or *to someone)*—overtake; come equal with (*with* and *to* are equally possible)

When he joined the class, he had fallen behind the other students, but he soon caught up to them.

She was such a fast runner that no one could catch up with her.

8. *cream of the crop*—the very best

In his high school, all his teachers thought he was the cream of the crop. They always knew he'd go far in the world.

Barry won't get married easily. He wants the cream of the crop.

9. *keep someone from (+ V + ing)*—prevent

Parents try to keep their children from getting into trouble.

Jane's boss kept her from going on vacation until the crisis was solved.

10. *show off (something)*—(S) attract attention to oneself or one's belongings, usually impolitely

Every time he buys a new car, he has to show it off.

Nobody likes her because she shows off her things too much.

11. *be up against*—be in competition with (also *go* up against)

He was up against some talented people when he won the contest.

Our candidate went up against tough competition in the last election.

12. *get back at someone*—get revenge (compare with *get even with*)

> You can't get back at everyone who hurts you.
> My best friend played a terrible joke on me, but I'll get back at her.

13. *keep up (with someone)*—go at the same speed

> It was hard for Steve to keep up with his friends because of his hurt foot.
> Kim is so smart that it's hard to keep up with her when she's planning something.

14. *have two strikes against one*—have a difficulty that makes success unlikely (notice it does not have to be two difficulties; this comes from baseball terminology—three strikes and you're out)

> Ted said he had been thinking about marrying Hilda, but she had two strikes against her; he wanted to marry a woman who could get a good job, and Hilda doesn't earn much.
> I would've loved to study engineering when I was in college, but I had two strikes against me. Engineering depends a lot on mathematics, and I can't understand mathematics at all.

15. *fair and square*—with justice; not cheating

> Everybody thought Joe and his wife got their apartment because they pulled strings. But they insist that they got it fair and square.
> I didn't steal this car. I got it fair and square. My brother moved to Chicago and left it with me.

16. *get a/the jump on (someone or something)*—get an immediate advantage, start ahead of time (*a* and *the* are equally possible)

> I was going to apply for the job as assistant manager, but Ted got the jump on me. He moved faster than I did.
> Pam got a jump on everyone else when she made her airplane reservations so early. I hear prices are going up now.
> I got a jump on my research paper by beginning my research a month ahead of time.

Check It Out

Take a closer look at the conversation from the "Zero In" section if you want to see any words or phrases that you might not have understood.

Election Surprise

Lisa: I can't believe Smith is going to quit the race for president. The election is just next month.

Alex: I don't think she has any choice. She had to take herself **out of the running** after that newspaper story about her.

Lisa: But that story was about something that happened almost 20 years ago. How do you think the newspapers found out about it?

Alex: That's obvious. One of her opponents told them.

Lisa: You think one of the other candidates gave the story to the newspaper?

Alex: Sure. Smith was winning the race and someone else didn't want to lose. He wanted to get her **out of his way**. It looked like she was going to do so well in the election that nobody would be able to **get the better of** her.

Lisa: You might be right. I remember when the campaign first started. She was so far behind that it looked like she would never **catch up to** the others. Nobody paid serious attention to her campaign. But later, she looked so good that somebody was afraid to **go head to head with** her.

Alex: Yeah, she **got a jump on** all the other candidates after that long story about her in the newspaper.

Lisa: I remember that, now. It was a very positive story. And right after that, her popularity increased a lot. Now all of that is lost. I wonder who was so worried about her winning?

Alex: I don't know. I always said she was the **cream of the crop**, the best candidate of that whole crowd. Now it looks like dirty tricks are going to decide the election. I guess she didn't realize what kind of people she **was up against**. The competition was stronger than she thought.

Lisa: Nowadays, nobody likes to win **fair and square**. Everybody is more interested in winning with tricks. What do you think she'll do now?

Alex: If I were her, I'd try to **get even with** the person who did this. She should find out who it is and then make sure he or she loses too.

Lisa: She can't do that! And I don't think she should do that. Do you really want elected officials who are only interested in revenge, **getting back at** all the people who cause trouble for them?

Alex: Not really. I'm just so angry. She would have been wonderful. Whoever did this to her wasn't even brave enough to attack her **face to face**. He had to let the newspapers do his dirty work for him.

Lisa: Well, it worked. That story in the newspaper was just enough to **keep her from** winning. It put an end to her campaign.

Alex: Who will you vote for now?

Lisa: I don't know. I guess I have to choose between Bates and Hammond.

Alex: What a choice. Both of them spend all of their time **showing off**. They're always telling everyone how wonderful they are.

Lisa: Maybe I should vote for Anderson. I like him.

Alex: Me too. But he **has two strikes against** him.

Lisa: What do you mean?

Alex: I agree that he's very good, but he has one big problem. He can't win because he's not very well known. Without name recognition, I don't think anybody can win.

Lisa: You're right. He doesn't have as much money as the other candidates, so he's had trouble **keeping up with** them in television advertisements. But we can still vote for him.

Creativity

13

"Necessity is the mother of invention."

This expression points out that we become our most creative when our need is the greatest. Bigger problems need more creative solutions. Can you think of some examples? This expression exists in many languages. Can you translate it from your language?

Get Ready

Prepare to hear a conversation by looking at the picture to the left and discussing the questions below with your teacher.

1. What are the three people interested in?
2. Why do you think they might be interested in it?

Get the Gist

Answer these questions after you listen to the conversation one time.

The New Home

1. What recently completed project are the speakers discussing?
2. Why was the project not as expensive as it might have been?
3. What was the problem with the kitchen? How was it solved?
4. Who was the architect?

Zero In

Determine the meanings of this chapter's idioms by listening to the conversation again and circling the most likely meaning for each idiom.

1. *fix it up*	plan	make pretty	build
2. *put our heads together*	consider solutions	kiss	compare
3. *came up with*	traveled	discovered	invited
4. *make do with*	force	buy	manage with less
5. *made up*	created	disliked	sold

6. *hit on*	discovered	argued	beat
7. *make that breakthrough*	cause damage	make a passage	find a solution after long work
8. *kick around*	hurt	discuss	change locations
9. *work out*	develop	get a job	be busy
10. *thought up*	created	considered	approved
11. *drawn up*	made a picture	taken a photograph	planned the details
12. *take shape*	make a decision	develop into the final form	become expensive
13. *dry run*	exercise	difficulty	practice
14. *dream up*	think about	learn about	create
15. *lost her touch*	became handicapped	lost a creative ability	became more creative

Get Your Bearings

Use these exercises to become familiar with the idioms. You may want to refer to the definitions and examples at the end of this chapter while you do them.

Exercise 1: You are a teacher and are trying to teach your students how to be more creative. The problem is that your students think creativity is immediate, and they get frustrated when they don't come up with creative ideas right way.

Using the idioms below, write an explanation to your students about the general stages of the creative process. (Note: Many of the idioms have the same meaning. You will often have several choices.)

come up with   **put their heads together**   **take shape**

kick them around   **think up**   **dream up**

Stage 1: Brainstorming

In this stage, you try to _____ as many ideas as you possibly can. It's usually much easier to brainstorm if you have a lot of people to

_____. That way, you can _____

_____.

It's also important not to reject any of the ideas that you _____ during this stage. Brainstorming depends a lot on having the freedom to

_____ even the most ridiculous possibilities.

hit on   **make a breakthrough**   **take shape**

make do with   **lose one's touch**

Stage 2: Illumination

This is the exciting stage where you _____ "the answer."

Some people even _____ during their sleep or when they're thinking about something completely different. At first, you may have only a vague idea of your solution. But the more you think about it, the more your idea begins

to _____ and become real.

fix up	**draw up**	**make do with**
work out	**dry run**	**work out**
dry run		

Stage 3: Adding Details and Evaluating

After you get your idea, it's time to _____ the problems and

other details. At this stage, some people like to _____ plans for implementing their idea. This is also a good time to check that you have the

necessary materials. If you don't, you'll have to get them or _____

_____ the materials that you already have. If you want to make

sure that you succeed, you might want to have a _____ to make sure that it works.

Exercise 2: Choose the professional who is most likely to do each action described below *as a regular part of the job*.

_____ *1.* work out plans
   a. a taxi driver
   b. a portrait painter
   c. an architect

_____ *2.* have a dry run
   a. a surgeon
   b. an actor
   c. a bus driver

_____ *3.* have her work take shape gradually
   a. a sculptor
   b. a stock broker
   c. an accountant

_____ *4.* lose his touch
   a. a gardener
   b. a window washer
   c. a filing clerk

_____ 5. kick around ideas
    a. waiters
    b. bank tellers
    b. advertising writers

_____ 6. make a breakthrough
    a. a cancer researcher
    b. an office receptionist
    c. a hair stylist

_____ 7. fix something up
    a. a hair stylist
    b. a television repairperson
    c. a waiter

_____ 8. make something up
    a. an accountant
    b. a surgeon
    c. a fashion designer

_____ 9. make do with some things
    a. a typist
    b. a cook
    c. a bus driver

_____ 10. put their heads together
    a. bank tellers
    b. office receptionists
    c. physicians

Follow-Up: The directions for this exercise asked you to choose the professionals who did the actions as a regular part of their jobs. Can you imagine the other professionals listed here doing the same actions occasionally? How?

Ⓡ **Exercise 3:** Your high school teacher assigned you to write about an invention and you chose the "hot dog" as your topic. You had typed it beautifully and set it on a table in your house. Unfortunately, your dog got it and chewed it apart. Now you have to figure out the order of the sentences. (Your dog is very clever. He only chewed *between* sentences!)

Number the following sentences in the order in which they should appear. The first one is done for you. Hint: Read all of the sentences before beginning.

*The Invention of the Hot Dog**

_____ He lost so many of them that he almost went broke trying to replace them.

_____ He thought about his problem for a long time when he hit on a solution.

* Based on *Seeds of Greatness*, by Denis Waitley, Pocket Books, 1983.

_____ The next day, he served the knockwurst inside the rolls and explained to his customers that they would have to do without the cotton gloves from now on.

_____ However, his gloves kept on disappearing.

__1__ Around 1930, a German immigrant was making a living in Philadelphia by selling knockwurst and sauerkraut.*

_____ To work out the problem, he thought up the idea of putting the knockwurst inside a German roll.**

_____ In time, it dawned on him that his customers were taking the gloves for working in their gardens, so he made up his mind to put an end to that.

_____ And from then on, the sandwich was known as the "hot dog."

_____ He made up a lot of these German rolls and cut them lengthwise.

_____ Because he didn't have enough money to buy plates and forks, he came up with the idea of giving his customers cheap cotton gloves to hold the knockwurst.

_____ But one of the customers looked around, saw the owner's dog sitting in the corner, and said, "Now we know why you dreamed up these rolls—to cover your knockwurst! What happened to the other dog that used to be here?"

_____ Most of the customers made do with the rolls just fine.

Tune In

Improve your ability to hear and understand idioms by listening to several short lectures and answering the questions below T for True or F for False.

You will hear several accounts of the creative processes of some well-known people.

A. (Pablo Picasso—artist)

_____ *1.* Pablo Picasso tried to plan each detail of his paintings before he began.

_____ *2.* Picasso claimed that he sometimes had to make do with colors that he didn't prefer.

_____ *3.* When Picasso was not satisfied with a painting, he destroyed the painting.

_____ *4.* One could say that Picasso's creations occurred gradually.

B. (Wolfgang Amadeus Mozart—composer)

_____ *5.* Mozart usually came up with his music when he and his partner put their heads together.

_____ *6.* Mozart usually drew up entire musical compositions in his head.

* Knockwurst is a German meat shaped like a big hot dog. Sauerkraut is sour cabbage.
** A roll is an individual-sized loaf of bread appropriate for sandwiches.

_____ 7. When Mozart tried to put his music on paper, he often still had to work out a lot of little problems.

_____ 8. It seems safe to say that Mozart followed a very analytical approach to composing.

C. (Henri Poincare—mathematician)

_____ 9. Poincare made his discoveries about Fuchsian functions after he had spent a lot of time working on his project.

_____ 10. Poincare made one of his discoveries after he was hit by a bus.

_____ 11. Poincare seems to have made his most important breakthroughs when he wasn't thinking about his work.

_____ 12. Poincare's experience seems to tell us that a change of environment can interfere with the creative process.

Get Down to Business

Improve your ability to use this chapter's idioms in conversation with a couple of your classmates by acting out one or more of the roleplays below.

1. (2 friends or co-workers)

You've been working on developing a new product (you choose the product) in your spare time that you're sure will be received very well by the world market. But you're not quite satisfied with it yet. It doesn't look very good, and it didn't work quite as well as you had hoped when you tried it. You are discussing the problem with a friend or co-worker, who is amazed that you were able to be so creative.

Use the following idioms in your discussion:

fix up	**come up with**	**make up**
hit on	**work out**	**take shape**
dream up	**dry run**	

2. (3 business people at a meeting)

Your company is planning to introduce a new product (you choose the product) and you are leading the design team. Today, you are meeting with two top executives in your company to explain the purpose and progress of your new product and to convince them they should approve further research and development of the project.

Use the following idioms in your discussion:

make do with	**come up with**	**make up**
take shape	**hit on**	**put (our) heads together**
think up	**draw up**	
fix up	**work out**	

3. (husband, wife, and interior designer)

You and your spouse are going to have a baby in a few months. You want to convert one of the rooms in your home into a nursery for your child. Now you are consulting with an interior designer to create a beautiful, comfortable, and functional room for your baby that doesn't cost too much money. The designer, who did a very nice job for your friends, needs to find out your preferences.

Use the following idioms in your discussion:

dream up	**work out**	**make do with**
kick around	**think up**	**fix up**
take shape	**put (our) heads together**	**come up with**
draw up		
	(not) lose one's touch	

4. (a student and a teacher)

You have been taking a fiction-writing course in which you've been working on a short story. Your teacher believes that you have a lot of writing talent and has suggested that you enter your completed story in a national contest after you first read it aloud to a group of students and teachers at your school. The problem is that you can't think of a good way to end your story, and there are some other technical problems with it. Your teacher tries to reassure you that you will be able to complete the story and suggests that you discuss it with someone.

Use the following idioms in your conversation:

dream up	**work out**	**dry run**
think up	**hit on**	**kick around**
make up	**fix up**	**put (our) heads together**
come up with		

Put It All Together

Reinforce your ability to speak using many of the idioms you've learned so far by acting out one or more of the roleplays below with your classmates.

7. (inventor and 2–3 corporate executives)

You have invented a wonderful new product (you decide what kind) that is years ahead of any similar product offered by other companies, and now you need a company to finance its production. You are trying to convince two (or three) executives from the XYZ company that your product will make their company extremely successful. They, however, are "bottom line" people; that is, they are mainly interested in finances and schedules. You not only must introduce them to the purpose of your product, but also must convince them that their company will make a lot of money pretty quickly if they produce it before the competition does. This is not immediately obvious, so you'll have to explain carefully. Recently, their company has not been doing well financially.

Use the following idioms in your discussion:

come up with	**make a breakthrough**	**(not) make do with**
hit on something	**carry out**	**fall behind**
around the clock	**run (cost)**	**in the red**
break even	**lay off**	**in the long run**
be about to	**bring up to date**	**bring up to date**
get a jump on		**read between the lines**

2. (2 creative persons and their business manager)

Your job is to be creative (fashion? music? dance? writing?). Your business manager's job is to set schedules, keep track of money, and make sure you follow the rules. In short, your goals are exactly the opposite, and sometimes this causes problems between you. Your manager wants you to follow schedules, pay more attention to your money, and obey the rules of the people who hire you. You believe that doing these things interferes with your "creative juices."

Use the following idioms as you discuss your differing opinions:

make a breakthrough	**think up**	**draw up**
hit on	**come up with**	**lose one's touch**
keep track of	**behind schedule**	**bring up to date**
go by the book	**call the shots**	**make ends meet**
do without	**make do with**	**make a living by**
go broke	**get out of line**	

3. (2 parents, son or daughter)

While you were in college, you became involved in music. You believe you have a lot of talent. You learned to play several instruments, you write songs, and you've been singing with a very successful rock band. You've been successful enough so far that you're sure you want to continue singing. However, your parents want you to go to graduate school so that you'll have a "nice, solid career" in business or medicine. They believe it's too hard to be really successful in music. You think this would be boring. You're only happy when you're making music. You try to explain to your parents.

Use the following idioms in your discussion:

come up with	**make up**	**make a breakthrough**
work out	**take shape**	**be broke**
right away	**make good as**	**miss out on**
play by ear	**have one's heart set on**	**make the most of**
make up one's mind		**be up against**
think twice about	**not stand a chance (of)**	**strike out**

4. (3–4 executives from 2 different companies)

You are having a meeting about a crisis that's developed: Both of your companies have developed an almost identical product (you choose) and are about to introduce it to the public. Each company was counting on being the only one to offer this product. You each believe that the other company had "insider" information about your company's plans: in other words, a corporate spy. Now you are angrily accusing the other of cheating and defending yourself from the accusation. You created this new product yourself, without cheating.

Use the following idioms in your discussion:

come up with	**draw up**	**work out**
dry run	**get even with**	**go head to head with**
get back at	**fair and square**	**go to any length**
one way or the other	**on purpose**	**once and for all**
waste one's breath	**be up for grabs**	**get to the bottom of**
	take someone at his word	

Keep the Ball Rolling

Get still more practice with the idioms you've learned so far by participating in a discussion.

In a group of three or four persons, try to solve the following problem. There are nine dots below. Draw no more than four straight lines *(without lifting your pencil from the paper)* that will cross *all nine dots.*

You should elect one person in your group "secretary" to take notes on the strategies all members of your group use to solve the problem. After you finish, suc-

cessfully or not, report the strategies you used to the class, using the idioms
below.*

●   ●   ●

●   ●   ●

●   ●   ●

work out	think up	hit on
kick around	make up	make a breakthrough
come up with	dawn on	put our heads together
figure out	do over	
give up (on)	make sure	no matter
to get (something)	go by the book	strike out

**Put a
Fine Point
on Them**

Use the following definitions and examples to help you understand the details of
this chapter's idioms when you do the exercises.

1. *dream up*—(S) create in a very imaginative way

   Mike dreamed up a delicious new dessert.
   That author dreamed a story up that people will love. It's so much fun.

2. *work out*—
   a. (S) to develop
      The architects worked magnificent plans out for a downtown office building.
      We've worked out an experimental plan that should get us a large grant.
   b. (Int.) be successful
      I hope your new job works out for you. It sounds wonderful.
      Phil tried living in Arizona for a few months, but it didn't work out.

3. *a dry run*—practice, a rehearsal

   Let's have a dry run before the concert. Then we won't be so nervous.
   Actors like to have a dry run before they begin a performance.

4. *lose one's touch*—lose a creative ability

> Arsenio was a great poet, but he seems to be losing his touch. Nobody has liked his last few poetry collections.
> Linda was a successful burglar until she got caught. I guess she just lost her touch.

5. *make do with (something)*—manage with less than is usually necessary

> We've run out of milk. I'll have to make do with water in this recipe.
> Joan couldn't afford a TV, so she made do with a radio to find out the news.

6. *think up*—create in an analytical way

> Sally thought up a clever story for her writing class. Everyone loved it.
> I have trouble thinking up places to take my relatives when they visit.

7. *hit on (something)*—find suddenly (used in discussing solutions to problems)

> The city thinks it's hit on a solution to the unemployment problem.
> Nano's hit on a way to learn English without studying! Are you interested?

8. *kick around (something)*—(S) discuss ideas as part of the creation or problem-solving process

> The design team kicked around a number of ideas before it settled on the proposed design.
> Conrad and his wife kicked several possibilities around before deciding on lasagna for the main course at their dinner party.

9. *make up (something)*—(S) invent; make by hand

> Becky has made up some wonderful stories to tell her students.
> Let's make up pretty cards for all of the children.

10. *draw up (something)*—(S) plan in detail, usually on paper

> Our architect drew up a very clever design for our new house.
> The program director is going to draw up a proposal to expand the children's center.

11. *fix up (something)*—(S) decorate; make more attractive or useful

> Fred fixed his new office up with photos of his wife and children.
> We fixed up our small apartment so that it looks like a livingroom in the daytime and a bedroom at night.

12. *take shape*—develop gradually into the final form, evolve

> After working for months, my novel was finally starting to take shape.
> It's very exciting to see a theatrical production take shape.

13. *make a breakthrough (on something)*—find a solution after great difficulty

> After a great deal of research, the scientist made the breakthrough on the molecular composition of the main compound.
> The medical team is rushing to make a breakthrough before it runs out of funds.

14. *put our heads together*—work together to create or find a solution (compare with *kick around*)

> We really wanted to impress our teacher, so we put our heads together and wrote a song.
> Separately, the chemists couldn't figure out the formula. Finally, they put their heads together and figured it out.

15. *come up with (something)*—create after long work; find something special after difficulty

> Jim came up with a story that made all of us laugh.
> The costume Jane wore to the party was great. How do you think she came up with it?

Check It Out

Take a closer look at the conversation from the "Zero In" section if you want to see any words or phrases that you might not have understood.

The New Home

Jenny: You certainly do have a beautiful home. But how did you two find the time to **fix it up** so nicely? You've really made it look beautiful.

Karen: Thanks, but we needed a professional to help us. For example, we hired an architect to help us change the structure of the rooms.

Tom: Right. Karen, the architect, and I **put our heads together** to discuss what we wanted and what was possible. After a few meetings, we **came up with** some very good ideas that everybody agreed with. The architect was very good at helping us discover what could be done.

Jenny: But it must've been pretty expensive, wasn't it?

Karen: Architects aren't cheap, that's for sure. But the rest of it was surprisingly inexpensive. Many times, we didn't even have to buy materials. We were able to **make do with** the materials we already had.

Tom: Yeah. For example, many of the curtains we have on the windows were made from bed sheets that we already had. In fact, Karen even **made up** some of the pillows on the couch from sheets.

Jenny: What an interesting idea.

Karen: The real problem was the livingroom. It was really small and not at all special. It just looked like a box. But finally, **we hit on** an idea after talking about it. The architect suggested adding a fireplace. That makes the room look bigger and gives it more character. We were really happy to **make that breakthrough**. That solution makes the livingroom look wonderful.

Tom: I have to admit, we were pretty frustrated about the livingroom at first. But it's funny how people can find solutions after they **kick something around** for a while. Talking about it really helps.

Jenny: Well, the fireplace is just wonderful. You **worked out** a beautiful solution. And I also love the windows in your diningroom. Were they here when you moved in?

Tom: No. That's another idea the architect **thought up**. She wanted to make the diningroom seem bright and charming. She said adding colored glass windows would do that for us.

Jenny: Did you make all of these plans ahead of time?

Karen: Oh yes. The architect had already **drawn up** plans for us to approve before work began. But it's funny. No matter how much we planned, it was so exciting when the house finally started to **take shape**. Seeing the result was much more exiting than seeing the plans.

Jenny: Could you tell me your architect's name? I might want to make a few changes in my house.

Tom: Here's her business card. She's actually just graduated recently.

Jenny: You're kidding. Was your house her first project?

Karen: Yes, it was. We knew her while she was a student. We wanted some work done and she needed to develop her reputation, so she used our house as a **dry run**. She got some extra practice, and we can show all our friends, like you, how good she was.

Jenny: Well I'm very impressed with her work. I can't wait to talk with her and find out what wonderful things she can **dream up** for my house. She seems to have a great imagination. I just hope she hasn't **lost her touch** already. I want some of that creativity she used on your house for myself.

Control

■ *"Hold your horses!"*

Very simply, this means "control yourself" or "wait a minute." Do you think it's a polite or formal expression? Who can you say this to? When might you want to say it?

Get Ready   Prepare to hear a conversation by looking at the picture to the left and discussing the questions below with your teacher.

1. What are the books on the table about?
2. Why do you think these books are on the table?
3. What do you think these people are discussing? Do they look like they agree?

Get the Gist   Answer these questions after you listen to the conversation one time.

Our World and Its Problems

1. Why is Ted upset?
2. What two opposing opinions do Carol and the men give about the government's role in the problem with the ozone layer (the greenhouse effect)?
3. What two opposing opinions do Carol and the men give about the government's role in decisions to have children?

Zero In   Determine the meanings of this chapter's idioms by listening to the conversation again and circling the most likely meaning for each idiom.

1. *keeping an eye on*	paying attention to	reading	criticizing
2. *keep tabs on*	watch carefully	receive	understand
3. *take charge of*	pay for	take control over	criticize
4. *take in hand*	take power or control over	follow	become angry

5. *gotten out of hand*	been uncontrolled	been too expensive	been unclear
6. *keep everyone in line*	control them	imprison them	put them in consecutive order
7. *takes them over*	gives a ride	helps	assumes control
8. *keep a lid on*	stop from increasing	spend money	increase
9. *puts its foot down*	refuses	makes plans	reconsiders
10. *won't stand for*	will remain seated	will be inactive	will not permit
11. *checking up on you*	helping financially	investigating	disagreeing
12. *are at the mercy of*	are helpful	are angry	are completely under another's power
13. *go off the deep end*	protect people	lose all control	become very involved
14. *lose track of*	put in the wrong place	make a mistake	not have information about
15. *got carried away*	traveled	lost all self-control	were robbed

---

Get Your Bearings

Use these exercises to become familiar with the idioms. You may want to refer to the definitions and examples at the end of this chapter while you do them.

Exercise 1: Read each statement and write T if it is True or F if it is False.

_____ 1. Most elementary school teachers would like their students to get out of hand.

_____ 2. Corporations would be grateful if governments took them over.

_____ 3. New parents who leave their children with a babysitter for an evening are likely to check up on the child by telephone.

_____ 4. A hostage is at the mercy of the terrorist who captures him.

_____ 5. Someone who suddenly wins a lot of money might get carried away.

_____ 6. Parents ought to put their foot down if their child decides to go to college.

_____ 7. People who lose track of their bank accounts don't make good money managers.

_____ 8. A company manager who won't stand for advice is probably a good manager.

____ 9. Someone who often goes off the deep end would be a good lawyer.

____ 10. It's a good idea to keep tabs on old friends.

____ 11. A parent has to put her foot down sometimes.

____ 12. A good manager will take people in hand when they aren't doing their jobs well.

____ 13. A politician would probably like to keep a lid on any stories that would embarrass him.

____ 14. Good leaders usually don't want to take charge.

____ 15. Parents shouldn't stand for their children's disobeying them.

Exercise 2: Choose the best idiom to complete each sentence below.

1. "Honey, I want to take a bath. Would you mind ____ the children for an hour or so?"

   a. being at the mercy of
   b. keeping an eye on
   c. getting carried away with

2. "My goodness. Look at all the things you bought today. You really ____, didn't you?"

   a. went off the deep end
   b. put your foot down
   c. took charge

3. "Oh no! I ____ the time. I'm supposed to be downtown in only 5 minutes."

   a. got carried away with
   b. lost track of
   c. kept track of

4. "I think we need to start our own labor union. Without a union, we'll always ____ our bosses."

   a. keep a lid on
   b. check up on
   c. be at the mercy of

5. The company president is very worried because a larger corporation seems to be planning to ____ our company.

   a. take over
   b. check up on
   c. be at the mercy of

6. One job of an elementary school teacher is to ____.

   a. lose track of the children
   b. take the childlren over
   c. keep the children in line

7. Many of her advisors tried to convince the prime minister to hold nationwide elections earlier than expected, but she _____.

   a. wouldn't stand for it
   b. took them over
   c. got out of hand

8. At the end of the trial, when the defendant was found guilty, he became very violent. The police had to be called in order to _____.

   a. check up on him
   b. be at his mercy
   c. take him in hand

9. After someone is released from prison, the authorities _____ him occasionally to be sure that he can establish a good life and won't get into trouble again.

   a. keep a lid on
   b. lose track of
   c. check up on

10. Because the people participating in the last protest march _____, more than one hundred police officers have been called for the next march.

    a. got out of hand
    b. put their foot down
    c. kept everyone in line

Ⓡ **Exercise 3:** Following is a story about a neighborhood's plan for a children's park. Read each sentence and find an idiom in the list that will not change the meaning of the sentence if it is substituted for the underlined words in each sentence. Write the letter on the line.

a. been had	**f. keep on**	**k. for good**
b. hit on something	**g. keep a lid on them**	**l. get carried away**
c. go head to head with	**h. get back at**	**m. doesn't stand for it**
d. keep tabs on	**i. come up with**	**n. take charge**
e. put their heads together about	**j. go to any length**	**o. give them a hand**

_____ *1.* Every Saturday, parents bring their young children to the park and keep an eye on their children while talking with friends.

_____ *2.* The time that the children spend in the park is an important release for them because all week their teachers try to keep them in line at school.

_____ *3.* Whenever the children become a little noisy or disobedient, their teacher puts her foot down.

_____ *4.* Of course, children are not known for their self-control. Sometimes, they really do go off the deep end.

_____ *5.* That's why the teachers have to take over and get the children involved in activities that will hold their interest.

_____ 6. Sometimes, though, it can be very hard to <u>think up</u> new and interesting activities for the children.

_____ 7. That's why the parents felt like they'd <u>made a real breakthrough</u> when they convinced the city to build a new park last year.

_____ 8. For a long tine, there had been very little for the children of the neighborhood to do on weekends, so the parents <u>kicked around</u> the problem with their city council representative.

_____ 9. The representative didn't like the idea at first because the city had limited money. The children's park had to <u>go up against</u> a new parking lot in the shipping district.

_____ 10. Eventually, the parents convinced the representative to <u>help them out</u>.

_____ 11. But then, they heard on the television news that the representative was supporting the parking lot instead. They had <u>been double-crossed</u>.

_____ 12. They decided to <u>get even with</u> the representative by talking to television reporters about their park and about how the representative had lied to them.

_____ 13. The representative said that everything had been a mistake, that the city would <u>not give up on</u> planning the park for the children.

_____ 14. In fact, while the television cameras were rolling, the representative promised to "personally <u>make sure</u>" to build the park.

_____ 15. The representative promised that the children of the city would come first <u>from now on</u> and that the children would soon have their park.

Ⓡ *Tune In*

Improve your ability to hear and understand idioms by listening to several short lectures and answering the questions below T for True or F for False.

A. (the common cold)

_____ 1. A scientist in Salisbury, England, has shown that emotional health is entirely separate from physical health.

_____ 2. According to this passage, the average person suspected the connection between emotional and mental health before scientists and doctors did.

_____ 3. In the Salisbury study, scientists must wait a long time for patients to catch a cold naturally.

_____ 4. According to a large study, there is no effect on the severity of a disease when the patient has few friends or family members.

_____ 5. People who have a positive view of life have a better chance of controlling their diseases.

B. (high school peer counseling)

_____ 6. The program discussed in this passage was created to reward those teenagers who have been responsible at home and at school.

_____ 7. Schools should typically choose the most intelligent or most popular students to be peer counselors.

_____ 8. According to the passage, students don't like to talk to adults about their problems because they see adults primarily as authority figures.

_____ 9. Peer counselors are taught to take charge of a difficult situation immediately.

_____ 10. Unfortunately, in Miami, Florida, peer counselors were not able to find out about problems that the teachers had already known about.

C. (overeating)

_____ 11. The typical overeater has tried a lot of different diets, but has experienced only temporary success.

_____ 12. Overeaters Anonymous has developed a special diet that is successful in most cases.

_____ 13. O.A. instructs members to watch each other very strictly to make sure that no member leaves his diet.

_____ 14. According to O.A., overeating is only a problem of self-control.

_____ 15. According to O.A., someone might be an overeater if he can control his eating behavior in front of other people but not when he's alone.

Get Down to Business

Improve your ability to use this chapter's idioms in conversation with a couple of your classmates by acting out one or more of the roleplays below.

1. (2–3 business partners)

You started a small business 3 years ago. (You choose the type of business.) One of you believes that the best way to expand the business is by buying a lot of equipment. The second believes that advertising is the key. The third believes that only by saving money will the business be strong. Recently, you've been having financial problems. Now you have to discuss your differing philosophies and the importance of controlling your spending; otherwise, the company will fail.

Use the following idioms in your discussion:

keep an eye on	**keep tabs on**	**get out of hand**
keep in line	**keep a lid on**	**put one's foot down**
not stand for	**lose track of**	**get carried away**
take over	**take charge of**	

2. (husband and wife)

Similar to the above situation, money troubles are destroying your budget and bank accounts. One of you loves to spend money on furniture, food, entertainment, clothing, appliances, etc. The other believes money was meant to be saved for future needs, not spent. Discuss your differing philosophies and the importance of controlling your spending.

Use the following idioms in your discussion:

go off the deep end	**keep a lid on**	**lose track of**
be at the mercy of	**keep someone in line**	**get out of hand**
take charge of	**put one's foot down**	**check up on**

3. (3 overeaters)

Two of you have been fighting overeating for several years. You have often spoken to each other to help each other avoid eating too much. Tonight, someone new is joining your discussion. This person has just recognized that overeating is ruining his or her life and wants help from the two of you. Together, you discuss what might cause the problem, how to fight it, and how all of you can help each other resist overeating.

Use the following idioms in your discussion:

take charge of	**take in hand**	**keep tabs on**
put one's foot down	**not stand for**	**lose track of**
get carried away	**be at the mercy of**	**check up on**
keep an eye on	**take over**	

4. (a babysitter and one or both parents)

You have just babysat one of the worst 2-year-olds you have ever met. That child was a monster all evening while the parents were at the symphony. (Make up some of the terrible things the child did to you!) Now the parents have arrived home, and they want to know how the evening was. You don't want to lose your babysitting job, but you want the parents to make some changes in the rules for these evenings—especially in their child's behavior.

Use the following idioms in your discussion:

keep an eye on	**keep tabs on**	**take in hand**
get out of hand	**keep in line**	**keep a lid on**
not stand for	**check up on**	**put one's foot down**
get carried away	**go off the deep end**	**be at the mercy of**

Put It All Together

Reinforce your ability to speak using many of the idioms you've learned so far by acting out one or more of the roleplays below with your classmates.

1. (5 or 6 neighbors)

Last week, there was a robbery in your neighborhood and all of you are nervous that your homes will be robbed next. You've decided to form a neighborhood "watch," an organization of neighbors in your area who will help to protect each other. As you discuss how to do this, it becomes clear that you fall into three groups:

The Passive Group: You think it's dangerous to get involved in crime protection. Instead of doing anything yourselves, you want to pressure the police to provide more protection for your neighborhood. You want absolutely nothing to do with guns; they're dangerous.

The Moderate Group: You want to do a few simple things to protect yourselves such as watch each other's homes, turn on outdoor lights, watch for strangers in the neighborhood, etc. You agree that more police help would be nice, but you know the police force is already very busy. You understand the attraction of guns, but you don't want one yourself.

The Radical Group: You don't think you can count on the police and you don't believe turning on lights, etc. is going to help. You think everyone should buy guns and learn how to use them. It's the only way to protect yourselves.

Use the following idioms as you discuss plans for your new organization:

keep an eye on	**keep tabs on**	**get out of hand**
keep a lid on	**not stand for**	**be at the mercy of**
make sure	**once and for all**	**take the bull by the horns**
be in the same boat	**take care of**	
draw up	**put (our or your) heads together**	**come up with**
take turns		**see eye to eye**
come through for	**pull together**	**scratch the surface**
go through proper channels	**help out**	**crack down on**
	the ins and outs	

2. (1 or 2 residents, 1 or 2 factory officials, and 1 or 2 government officials)

Resident(s): A factory in your neighborhood has been increasing the amount of air pollution. The smell is terrible, and you worry about the effects the air quality will have on yourselves and your families. Today, you are having a meeting to complain to the factory president (and vice president). You have invited (a) government representative(s) to the meeting also.

Factory official(s): If you agree to the residents' demands, you'll have to install expensive air quality control equipment. Besides, you don't think the air quality is very bad, and your scientists tell you that it is not dangerous.

Government official(s): You are most worried about winning the next election. These residents belong in your voting district, but the factory officials contributed a lot of money to your last election campaign. While you know the smell has been bad, the pollution has not exceeded government limits.

Use the following idioms during your meeting:

lose track of	**not stand for**	**be at the mercy of**
put one's foot down	**get out of hand**	**keep tabs on**
get across	**waste one's breath**	**get after**
get rid of	**gather from**	**get to the bottom of**
in time	**in the long run**	**from now on**
make sure	**keep on**	**no matter**
make up one's mind	**by all means**	**out of the question**
come up with	**put (our or your) heads together**	

3. (2 police officers and 2 noisy residents)

You've been called to a neighborhood where people complained that there's too much noise coming from one house. Your job as police officers is to convince them to be quieter so that the other neighbors can have a peaceful evening. It appears, however, that the noisy neighbors have been celebrating some good luck (you decide what) and have been drinking alcohol as part of their celebration. As a result, they're very hard to convince to be quiet.

Use the following idioms as all of you discuss this:

get out of hand	**keep in line**	**keep a lid on**
check up on	**go off the deep end**	**get carried away**
do a favor	**meet one halfway**	**give a break**
on the spur of the moment	**around the clock**	**put an end to**
	toe the line	**get along with**
put up with	**play by ear**	**put (our or your) heads together**

4. (3 small-business entrepreneurs)

The three of you are starting your first small business. (You decide the type of business.) Two of you believe one of the first purchases you absolutely must make is a good computer system. It will help you have an advantage over your competitors. But the third person has never used a computer and, in fact, is scared to death (very frightened) of them. This person believes that computers will one day take over the world, so he or she is dead set against (completely disagrees with) having a computer system in your business. You need to find a way to bring this person into the 20th century!

Use the following idioms in your discussion:

take over	**be at the mercy of**	**take charge of**
not stand for	**one way or the other**	**think twice about**
take into account	**draw the line at**	**get the jump on**
make sense of	**give a hand**	**bring up to date**
keep track of	**lose track of**	**for the time being**

Keep the Ball Rolling

Get still more practice with the idioms you've learned so far by participating in a discussion.

Debate: Childhood vs. Adulthood

If you had your choice, would you want to be a child again? Which is better: childhood or adulthood?

The purpose of a debate is to present your opinions logically and convince your listeners that your opinion is correct. Your teacher will divide your class into two teams: those who think childhood is better and those who think adulthood is better. You will be given time to plan the reasons for your opinion as a team and then you will present that opinion and answer the other team's opinion according to the following schedule.

Planning Period: 15 minutes
   Step A: List the reasons for your opinion
   Step B: Predict the other team's reasons and plan your arguments against
            them

Team #1: Present opinion and reasons   5 minutes
Team #2: Present opinion and reasons   5 minutes

Team #1: Argue against Team #2's opinions   3 minutes
Team #2: Argue against Team #1's opinions   3 minutes

Rules: Each person may speak for his team only one time and for no longer
       than 1 minute.

At the end, you may vote on which team was more successful.

Try to use the following idioms when you present your opinions:

not stand for	**keep in line**	**put one's foot down**
take charge of	**be in charge of**	**check up on**
be at the mercy of	**dream up**	**go head to head with**
be up against	**have two strikes against one**	**keep someone from**
take care of		**get to (+ Verb)**
take into account	**get after**	**know the ropes**

(continued)

make sense of

catch on to

have something going for one

get one's own way

Put a Fine Point on Them

Use the following definitions and examples to help you understand the details of this chapter's idioms when you do the exercises.

1. *Keep an eye on something or someone*—watch carefully; pay careful attention to

   The police are keeping an eye on that neighborhood because they were told a suspect is hiding there.
   A good babysitter has to keep an eye on the children all the time.

2. *lose track of something or someone*—lose knowledge about; not have a record of (contrast with *keep track of*, Ch. 2)

   I've lost track of most of my high school friends over the last 10 years.
   I keep a budget so that I don't lose track of my money.

3. *(not) stand for something*—(not) permit or allow; (not) tolerate (usually used in the negative)

   Our teacher won't stand for talking during class. He says it disturbs everyone.
   You shouldn't stand for your neighbor's noise every night. Call the landlord and complain.

4. *keep someone or something in line*—maintain control over something or someone (contrast with *get out of line*, Ch. 5)

   It's hard to keep very young children in line, especially when they're excited.
   The police managed to keep the protesters in line during their demonstration.

5. *put one's foot down*—refuse

   He wanted to stay with me for 6 months, but I put my foot down. He'll stay for 1 month instead.
   We asked for a retest, but the examiner put his foot down. He said it wasn't permitted.

6. *keep a lid on something*—control; stop from increasing

   The National Guard was asked to keep a lid on the riots in the Capitol.
   One of the things the president promised when she was a candidate was to keep a lid on tax increases.

7. *take over something*—(S) assume complete control, often without permission

   I wanted to run the meeting myself, but as usual Tom took over.
   The inmates took over the jail cafeteria and demanded better food.
   After Judy leaves, her duties will be taken over by two different people.

8. *take charge of something*—provide leadership; assume responsibility

   After Joe left, Mike took charge of the computer room.
   Ann wants to take charge of training the new employees, but the director doesn't think she's capable of that yet.

   be in charge of something—be the leader
   Carol is in charge of student advising for the institute.
   Abdullah was in charge of presenting the students' request to the director.

9. *check (up) on something*—investigate

> We went to the state capital to check up on my driver's license application.
> Would you please check on the status of my driver's license application?

10. *keep tabs on something or someone*—maintain knowledge of; maintain a record of (compare with *keep track of*, Ch. 2)

> The government keeps tabs on all people entering and leaving the country.
> Would you keep tabs on my house while I'm on vacation?

11. *take (someone or something) in hand*—establish control over someone or something to organize better

> After the earthquake, the Red Cross took the survivors in hand by finding them temporary housing and food.
> The new chief executive officer will take the corporation in hand at the beginning of the new year.

12. *be at the mercy of someone; be at one's mercy*—be completely under another's power or control; depend on completely

> If you don't have a lease for your apartment, you'll be at the mercy of your landlord. He can take the apartment from you at any time.
> One reason prisoners have trouble adjusting to the world after they are freed is because they spent so much time at their captors' mercy.

13. *get out of hand*—become uncontrolled

> Because the crowd in front of the store appeared to be getting out of hand, the manager called the police.
> Residents living near the airport complained to the city that the noise from the airplanes was getting out of hand.

14. *go off the deep end*—lose control over one's actions or emotions; do too much of something

> After Lucy won the lottery, she went off the deep end. She spent all the money within a month.
> Robert would have gone off the deep end when his wife died if his family hadn't given him so much support.

15. *get carried away (with something)*—lose control because of excitement or enthusiasm

> Joan thought the roses were so beautiful that she got carried away and bought six dozen of them.
> Don't get carried away with the sun while you're on the beach. You don't want to get a bad sunburn.

Check It Out

Take a closer look at the conversation from the "Zero In" section if you want to see any words or phrases that you might not have understood.

Our World and Its Problems

Bob: Hi, Ted, Carol. Hey, what's wrong with *you*, Ted?

Ted: I'm not in a very good mood. I have to do a research paper for my environmental studies class.

Bob: Can't you think of a topic?

Ted: That's my problem. I can think of too many topics. First there's the ozone layer and the greenhouse effect.

Bob: Yeah, that's a problem all right. We have to start **keeping an eye on** how much carbon dioxide we create. If we don't pay attention to that now, we'll all be sorry later.

Carol: I don't think we have to worry too much. The government will **keep tabs on** the problem. I mean they'll watch the problem and they'll **take charge of** the situation. They know how to control it.

Ted: You expect the government to **take in hand** all the corporations and owners of automobiles to protect the environment? I don't think so. The government isn't going to force people to be responsible for the environment until it's too late.

Carol: I disagree with you. First of all, the problem hasn't **gotten out of hand** yet. We still have plenty of time to control it. Second of all, I think we can depend on our elected government officials to **keep everyone in line,** corporations and automobile owners both. For example, the Environmental Protection Agency has thousands of employees who enforce environmental laws.

Bob: The only way the government could control the corporations is if it **takes them over**. Corporations are only interested in money, profit. Only if the government controls the corporations will they be environmentally responsible.

Carol: Well, we'll never agree with each other about this topic. What else are you considering writing about. Ted?

Ted: I was thinking about the overpopulation problem and its effects on the environment. You know, in some countries it's really a problem to find enough food, housing, and land for the people, but they continue to have more and more children.

Carol: I think that's another thing that the government can **keep a lid on**. If the government has enough advertising campaigns and educates its people, it can control the population.

Bob: But Carol, it's not as easy as that. In many countries, people have a lot of children because the culture says a person is rich when he has a lot of children. If the government simply **puts its foot down** and refuses to let them have a lot of children, the people will become extremely angry—in fact, they simply **won't stand for it**.

Ted: And I don't blame them. I wouldn't want the government telling me what to do. Would you like the government **checking up on you** all the time, making sure that you don't have more children than they'll permit you to have?

Carol: But sometimes it's just necessary, for the good of everyone. When people **are at the mercy of** their environment, when they depend on it so much, they have to be good to it. I don't think the government should **go off the deep end**, of course. I don't think population growth should be completely uncontrolled, but it does need to protect all people.

Bob: Who says what is too far? I think it is very easy to **lose track of** what the government is or is not doing. We should always know what our leaders are doing and not doing, and . . .

Ted: Guys! Hello? Remember me? I'm the guy who has to think of a research paper topic?

Carol: Sorry, Ted. I guess we **got carried away**. I always love a good argument. Let's try to control ourselves and help Ted find a topic.

Foolishness

15

"While the cat's away, the mice will play."

This popular expression says that people behave less correctly when they aren't being watched. We might use it to talk about work, school, or home life. Can you think of examples of the "mouse" playing while the "cat" is away? Does your language have an expression like this?

Get Ready

Prepare to hear a conversation by looking at the picture to the left and discussing the questions below with your teacher.

1. Where do you think these people are?
2. Why is the woman holding the clothes? What do you think she wants to do with them?
3. Do the men seem to agree with her?

Get the Gist

Answer these questions after you listen to the conversation one time.

A School Prank*

1. What relationship do these three people have?
2. Who is the woman angry at and why?
3. What does the woman want to do? How do the men feel about that?
4. In the end, what does each of them decide?

Zero In

Determine the meaning of this chapter's idioms by listening to the conversation again and circling the most likely meaning for each idiom.

1. *blew*	studied hard for	failed	forgot about
2. *cutting too many corners*	moving fast	working carelessly	working efficiently
3. *let us down*	remember us	permit us	disappoint us

* Trick.

4. *messed up*	did badly on	worked on	succeeded on
5. *goofing off*	working	sleeping	wasting time
6. *fooling around*	having fun	traveling	resting
7. *lost your head*	became sick	became wild	became less intelligent
8. *get in trouble*	be in a difficult situation	punish	solve problems
9. *getting on his nerves*	making him laugh	bothering him	hurting his health
10. *have a screw loose*	are foolish	are intelligent	are unhealthy
11. *make fun of*	enjoy	imagine	joke about
12. *knock it off*	stop it	hit it	signal at a door
13. *make waves*	create	cause trouble	tell a joke
14. *make a fool of*	trick	cause to appear silly	cause interest
15. *get caught red-handed*	be found while doing wrong	wash too many dishes	do work by hand
16. *get away with*	steal	disappear	do wrong without punishment

Get Your Bearings

Use these exercises to become familar with the idioms. You may want to refer to the definitions and examples at the end of this chapter while you do them.

Exercise 1: Read each statement below and write T for true or F for false.

_____ *1.* If you are running out of time, you might have to cut corners.

_____ 2. When you mess up your homework, you aren't likely to get a good grade on it.

_____ 3. You should make fun of your guests when you have a party.

_____ 4. Someone who loses his head will probably have to spend time in a psychiatric hospital.

_____ 5. You probably won't want to marry someone who gets on your nerves.

_____ 6. It's a good idea to fool around a little when you need a break from hard work.

_____ 7. Someone who has a screw loose could have to spend time in a psychiatric hospital.

_____ *8.* You aren't likely to want to spend time with someone who often makes a fool of you.

_____ 9. You should apologize to someone that you have let down.

_____ 10. You can get your work done faster if you goof off.

_____ 11. When you feel very hot, it helps to blow something.

_____ 12. Someone who tells you to "knock it off" probably enjoys your actions.

_____ 13. A thief who has gotten away with stealing a car hasn't been caught by the police yet.

_____ 14. Society always values people who makes waves.

_____ 15. When someone gets in trouble, he might be punished.

_____ 16. It's obvious that someone is guilty when he's been caught red-handed.

Exercise 2: For an assignment, your little sister was asked to write a letter to the leader of your country about her choice of problems. The teacher said her letter was too "informal" and "not polite enough." Help your sister to do this by writing more formal phrases above the underlined informal ones.

Dear President,

My teacher asked me to write a letter to you about a problem in our country, and I have chosen education. I think the biggest problem is that the school <u>cuts too many corners</u>. It just doesn't have enough money. Some of us don't have books for our classes, and we can't learn about computers because our school doesn't have any.

Another big problem is that the students <u>fool around</u> a lot. It seems like it's always the same students who <u>make waves</u> all the time, and the problem is that they <u>get away with it</u>, even when they're <u>caught red-handed</u>. This really <u>gets on my nerves</u>. I usually stay quiet, but sometimes I get so angry that I just tell everyone to <u>knock it off</u>. I think we need more teachers to keep everyone in line.

The last thing I want to talk about is your decision to reduce the amount of money the government gives for school sports programs. Your advisors must <u>have a screw loose</u>. How can you do that? It will only <u>mess up</u> everybody's lives more. In my school, if kids couldn't play sports after school, they would only go home and <u>goof off</u>. You really <u>blew it</u> when you made that decision, and I hope you will change soon. By the way, except for education, I think you are a good president.

Sincerely yours,

Patty

Exercise 3: You are an elementary school reading teacher, and you're trying to teach your young students good habits in a fun way. You've made up a bulletin board for the wall of your classroom. It will have the following illustrations, but you must come up with titles for each. Use the list of titles below.

Fooling Around

Getting Caught Red-handed

Getting on Her Nerves

Making Fun of Her

Losing His Head

Letting Them Down

Getting Away with It

Cutting Corners

Goofing Off

1. _____

_____

2. _____

_____

3. _____

_____

4. _____

_____

5. _____

_____

6. _____

_____

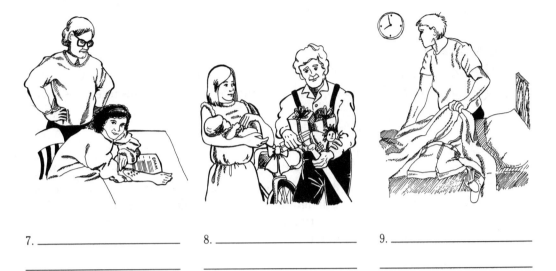

7. _____

_____

8. _____

_____

9. _____

_____

Tune In

Improve your ability to hear and understand idioms by listening to several conversations and answering the questions below T for True or F for False.

A. (2 friends)

_____ 1. The speaker's friend, Marty, is a flight attendant.

_____ 2. The flight was quiet and comfortable until a passenger pulled out a gun.

_____ 3. One of the passengers was shot.

_____ 4. The speakers believe that the passenger with the gun was probably arrested by the police later.

B. (2 friends)

_____ 5. The woman thinks her roommate is dangerous.

_____ 6. The woman's roommate doesn't care about having a clean home.

_____ 7. The woman is probably more angry with her roommate now than she was last week.

_____ 8. The man disagrees with the woman.

C. (2 co-workers)

_____ 9. The man has just finished speaking to a group at a meeting.

_____ 10. The man's speech went badly because the woman didn't help him enough.

_____ 11. The man and the woman like Mr. Washington.

_____ 12. Mr. Washington is planning to remove Marion Winston from her job.

_____ *13.* Marion Winston doesn't respect Mr. Washington.

_____ *14.* The man and woman plan to continue their project.

Get Down to Business

Improve your ability to use this chapter's idioms in conversation with a couple of your classmates by acting out one or more of the roleplays below.

1. (2 friends)

It's almost the end of your semester at school and final examinations are coming soon. One of you has been doing all of your reading and studying gradually all semester. But the other has been spending all his or her time going to parties, having fun, and laughing at you for working hard. Now it's time to study, and this person is very worried about grades. You are going to "have the last laugh" as your friend complains.

Use the following idioms in your conversation:

cut corners	**fool around**	**blow (something)**
get away with	**get in trouble**	**goof off**
make fun of	**have a screw loose**	**lose one's head**

2. (2–3 friends)

You are very worried about your friend. Your friend has been gambling too much lately; you're worried that it's a disease. Your friend spends a lot of money on the lottery (a government-run contest), goes to the racetrack, and travels to cities with casinos very often. You believe that your friend has been gambling so much that he or she doesn't have enough money to make ends meet and his family is suffering because of it. Tonight, you've invited your friend to dinner so that you can bring him or her around.

Use the following idioms in your discussion:

let down	**goof off**	**lose one's head**
get away with	**mess up**	**cut corners**
make a fool of	**knock it off**	**have a screw loose**
make waves	**fool around**	

3. (a teacher and 1 or 2 students)

You left your office in the school for a few minutes, and when you returned, you found one or two students looking at a test you were planning to give their class the next day (you choose the subject). Because you hadn't had an appointment with them, you believe that they had waited on purpose until you left your office so that they could get a look at the test. These students are usually unprepared for class. They say they were only looking for their homework assignments. You are very angry.

Use the following idioms in your discussion:

blow (something)	**get away with**	**get in trouble**
lose one's head	**have a screw loose**	**catch red-handed**
mess up	**cut corners**	**fool around**
knock it off	**make waves**	**let down**

4. (2 employees and the supervisor)

The two of you don't like your boss very much. You think that he or she isn't really smart enough to be the supervisor. In addition, your boss is a little over-weight and has a small speech impediment (a speaking problem). While you are taking your coffee break (15 minutes free from work), you begin discussing your supervisor and making fun of these problems. Later, your supervisor comes into the room while you are doing this and overhears some of it. Of course, the supervisor is very upset with you.

Use the following idioms in your conversation:

mess up	**goof off**	**make waves**
knock it off	**make a fool of**	**fool around**
catch red-handed	**make fun of**	**get on someone's nerves**
lose one's head	**have a screw loose**	**let down**

Put It All Together

Reinforce your ability to speak using many of the idioms you've learned so far by acting out one or more of the roleplays below with your classmates.

1. (1–2 bank credit officers and a husband and wife.)

The two of you have had a joint credit card with this bank for several years. The bank gives you a credit "line" of $3,000, which means you can buy $3,000 worth of merchandise at various stores. The bank pays the store for your purchases, and you pay the bank a certain amount of money every month until you have repaid the $3,000 and a percentage (usually 18%) in "interest" (extra money to "thank" the bank for letting you spend more money that you actually have!). Recently you've been having trouble making payments on this credit card because you have too many credit cards and you owe a *lot* of money to many banks and stores. You need to negotiate with the bank: You want to continue paying back the money that you owe, but you want to pay less each month. This will make your payments for all your credit cards more manageable. Of course, the bank prefers that you continue your regular payments.

Use the following idioms in your negotiations:

get in trouble	**lose one's head**	**mess up**
cut corners	**get out from under**	**live it up**
do without	**get out of hand**	**carry out**
catch up on	**lose track of**	**crack down on**
once and for all	**go off the deep end**	**keep a lid on**

2. (a husband and wife)

You are very angry with your spouse (the person you are married to). First, your spouse has been spending far too much money. Both of you work outside the home, and you've been trying to save enough money to buy a house. But lately, your spouse has been buying a lot of things (you decide what). In addition, your spouse hasn't been spending enough time at home recently, but instead has been going out with friends after work, sometimes staying out until very late. You believe your spouse is tired of saving all the money for the house. You need to strengthen your spouse's determination.

Use the following idioms in your conversation:

cut corners	**fool around**	**blow (something)**
let down	**come up in the world**	**do without**
toe the line	**get carried away**	**keep one's word**
get out of hand	**make up**	**put one's foot down**

3. (a police officer and 2 students)

You and your friend don't like the university president much because he's "stuffy": he dresses too formally, speaks too formally, and wears a stupid hat. Last night, the two of you spent a lot of time finding some clothes that looked very similar to the clothes the president of your college wears (except you had trouble with the hat, so you had to use one that was a little different). While you were putting them on the statue of the university's founder, a campus police officer drove by and caught you. Now you have to explain what you were doing and hope the police officer doesn't take you to jail! (Does the police officer like the president?)

Use the following idioms in your conversation:

catch red-handed	**make waves**	**show off**
make fun of	**fool around**	**dream up**
think up	**make do with**	**be at the mercy of**
fix up	**go by the book**	**(not) stand for**
put up with	**get rid of**	**from now on**

4. (a corporate official and 2 representatives from an advertising agency)

Your corporation has decided to stop using its current advertising agency because it feels they are not creative enough or hard-working enough. Some of the agency's best people have left in the past year, and the people who remain aren't good enough. Just last month, they submitted a strategy for an advertising campaign that was already being used by another company. Today you are informing them of your corporation's decision. Naturally, they won't be happy because your corporation was one of their biggest accounts.

Use the following idioms in your discussion:

cut corners	**let down**	**blow (something)**
count on	**make sure**	**on purpose**
do over	**lose one's touch**	**hit on**
put (our or your) heads together	**come up with**	**work out**
	make up one's mind	**be out of the running**
cut off		

Keep the Ball Rolling

Get still more practice with the idioms you've learned so far by participating in a discussion.

Imagine that you are the person indicated in the situations below. With some of your classmates, discuss the suggestions that you would make for one or both of these problems. Try to use the idioms indicated after each problem as you present your decisions.

1. (the principal of a high school)

One of the students in your school has become a problem since her brother died in a car accident 3 months ago. She used to be an average student, had an appropriate number of friends, behaved correctly in the classroom, and belonged to the Study Abroad club at school because she hoped to study in another country someday. But in the past few weeks, her grades have gone down, she hasn't been coming to class every day, she makes a lot of noise when she comes to class, and she has spent her time either alone or with some of the "tough" kids in the school. Her teachers are worried about her. What advice will you give her teachers? Will you talk to her parents? Will you talk to her? What will you say to them?

goof off	**mess up**	**fool around**
make waves	**take in hand**	**keep an eye on**
give the cold shoulder	**make friends with**	**take into account**
bring around	**come through for**	**check up on**
get to the bottom of	**scratch the surface**	**read between the lines**

2. (a co-worker)

You share an office with a co-worker. A few minutes ago, the department manager had been talking with you and your co-worker. When he left, he dropped some money. Your co-worker, who is also a good friend of yours, picked it up and put it in his pocket, saying "Finders, keepers."* He laughed and said that he planned to take his girlfriend out to a nice dinner at a good restaurant with the money. What should you do about it?

get away with	**get in trouble**	**lose one's head**
let down	**get after**	**bring around**
double-cross	**make sure**	**keep an eye on**
check up on	**go by the book**	**live it up**
figure out	**dawn on**	**catch on to (someone)**

Put a Fine Point on Them

Use the following definitions and examples to help you understand the details of this chapter's idioms when you do the exercises.

1. cut corners—do something incompletely or carelessly

Tim always cuts corners, so we rarely give him important jobs to do.
I cut so many corners during the semester that I was afraid I'd fail all my classes.

2. mess up—(S) ruin, spoil (also used: *screw up*)

You messed up my plans by arriving so early!
He messed his speech up when he forgot to discuss one of the most important points.

3. fool around—have fun, joke, play games; waste time; (also used: *mess around*)

I took your negative comments seriously, but Mike said you were just fooling around.
They lost their jobs because they were fooling around during working hours.

4. get on someone's nerves—annoy or bother someone

Would you please turn down the TV? That noise is getting on my nerves.
Her constant complaining is starting to get on my nerves.

5. to blow something—make a big mistake; ruin (compare with *mess up*)

I blew my chance to get that job when I told the interviewer I couldn't travel to other cities.
I just blew my test! I thought I knew everything, but I couldn't think of any of the answers.

6. get away with something—not be punished for wrongdoing

Everyone was surprised when Bill got away with not paying his parking tickets for a whole year. I'm surprised the police didn't arrest him!

---

* A popular saying when people find something and don't want to return it. "Finders, keepers; losers, weepers."

You always get away with coming to class late. Why doesn't the teacher get angry with you?

7. *get in trouble*—be punished for wrongdoing, put oneself in a difficult situation.

   I got in trouble when I tried to drive to the mountains without a map.
   You'd better do your homework or you'll get in trouble with your parents.

   get (someone) in trouble—put another person in a difficult position
   My assistant got me in trouble when he suggested that I had already known about the company's financial problems.

8. *knock it off*—command to stop doing something objectionable (not polite; usually said in anger)

   I was singing children's songs, but I guess it got on my roommate's nerves. She told me to knock it off.
   Bob accused us of telling lies and told us to knock it off.

9. *lose one's head*—lose self-control; become wild (compare with *get carried away* and *go off the deep end*, Ch. 14.)

   I'm sorry I drove so fast. I lost my head for a minute.
   He was so happy that he lost his head and bought dinner for everyone in the restaurant.

10. *goof off*—(Int.) waste time (compare with *fool around*)

    Weekdays are for working. Weekends are for goofing off.
    If you continue to goof off, you'll never get ahead.

11. *make fun of something or someone*—joke about unkindly, mock

    The children made fun of little Mary because she didn't know how to swim.
    Thirty years ago, parents made fun of rock music.

12. *have a screw loose*—be strange, foolish, or crazy

    Barbara wants to move to Antarctica. She must have a screw loose.
    He's been talking to himself in front of the mirror for a week. I think he has a screw loose.

13. *make a fool of someone*—cause someone to look foolish

    Why did you tell everyone I was too inexperienced to direct the project? You made a fool of me.
    Mildred made a fool of herself singing at the concert. Her voice is terrible.

14. *let down (someone)*—(S) to disappoint someone

    My parents were very upset when I wasn't accepted by their university. They said that I had let them down.
    I'm sorry to let down the company, but I won't be able to go to the conference next month.

15. *make waves*—cause trouble; make a process more difficult

    Children who make waves at school are punished.
    Todd tries to make waves at every meeting. As a result, our meetings are twice as long as they need to be.

16. *catch someone red-handed*—be found during the act of doing something wrong (occasionally used in a friendly way about an act of kindness)
    (+ Verb + -ing)

    June has been fired from her job because she was caught red-handed "borrowing" money from the company without permission.

The police officers insisted that they had been courteous while arresting the protestors, but a television news station caught them red-handed beating a protestor.

Terri, what beautiful flowers! Now, don't pretend you didn't bring them. We've caught you red-handed!

___

Check It Out

Take a closer look at the conversation from the "Zero In" section if you want to see any words or phrases that you might not have understood.

A School Prank

Kate: I really **blew** that test. Dr. Smith told me that he had never seen anybody get such a low grade on one of his tests. He was really angry.

Mike: What happened? You usually get pretty good grades.

Tim: I know what happened to her. She's been **cutting too many corners**. Ever since you got involved with that theater group, Kate, you haven't been paying as much attention to your school work.

Kate: Thanks, *Dad*! Really, Tim, you sound exactly like my father. "Now, Kate. We're glad you like the theater, but don't forget the most important thing is studying. Don't **let us down**."

Mike: You would be just as disappointed as your parents if you got low grades.

Kate: OK. But I only **messed up** one test. Now it looks like Dr. Smith is going to take me out of the theater group.

Mike: That doesn't sound fair. Why?

Kate: He says I'm **goofing off** too much. I tried to tell him that I'm not wasting time with the theater group. I want to go into theater as a career.

Tim: What did he say to that?

Kate: He doesn't think somebody *my age* can be serious about any career. I don't want to talk about this anymore. What are we going to do tonight?

Mike: We could go to the pizza shop and see if some of the guys are there.

Tim: That's old and boring. Any good movies in town?

Kate: That's boring too. Listen, I have an idea. I feel like **fooling around**. Nothing bad, but funny.

Tim: OK. We're listening.

Kate: You know that statue of the school's first president—old Dr. Hunter?

Mike: Yeah. What about it?

Kate: Well, it's winter, you know. And the poor guy has been wearing the same cold, metal clothes for a century at least. Let's put some clothes on him— the same kind of clothes Dr. Smith wears.

Tim: You're the one who's crazy! Have you **lost your head**? If Dr. Smith catches us, we'll really **get in trouble**. He might even throw us out of school.

Kate: Of course Smith will be angry. Half the fun of doing it is **getting on his nerves**. I can't wait to see the look on his face. And I'm so angry with him, I don't mind getting even.

Mike: I have to agree with Tim, Kate. I think you **have a screw loose** even to *think* about doing something like this.

Kate: No, guys, just listen. You know how Dr. Smith *always* wears the same brown suit, white shirt, and red tie? We could dress the statue of Dr. Hunter the same way!

Tim: You mean **make fun of** Dr. Smith by dressing the statue in the same colors? That *is* pretty funny, I have to admit. Everybody already laughs at the way the old guy dresses.

Mike: **Knock it off**, guys. You can't be seriously thinking about doing this. Its stupid anyway.

Kate: Don't tell me you're afraid to **make waves**. It doesn't mean we'll go to jail if we get caught. Anyway, I'm very angry at Dr. Smith and this is a really good chance to **make a fool of** him. Everybody will laugh at him.

Tim: Sounds like fun. How about you, Mike?

Mike: Nope. And when you guys **get caught red-handed**, don't ask me to help you out.

Tim: You worry too much. I know we can **get away with** it. Nobody'll see us at night.

Glossary

A

a dry run (13)—practice, a rehearsal

according to someone or something (5)—in the opinion of an expert or knowledgeable source

(all) add up (6) (Int.)—be understandable; be sensible or believable (uses inanimate subjects only)

ahead of time (1)—early; before the scheduled time (appears only at the end of a clause or sentence)

around the clock (2)—24 hours each day; continuously

B

back down (from something) (9)—stop arguing one's position

back out (of) (7)—change a decision or agreement that has already been made; remove support for a decision

back up (3) (S)—support another's position or opinion

be a steal (4)—be a very good bargain; be surprisingly cheap

be about to (2)—be almost ready to; be close to doing something (+ V)

be at the mercy of someone/be at one's mercy (14)—be completely under another's power or control; depend on completely

be had (11)—be cheated

be in charge of something (14)—be the leader

be in the running (12)—have a good chance to achieve something

be in the same boat (11)—have the same problem

be out of the running (12)—have no chance to achieve something

be up against (12)—be in competition with (also *go up against*)

be up for grabs (8)—be available to take

be up to (someone) (7)—be the decision of someone

be/go broke (4)—have no money

beat around the bush   (9)—make a point very indirectly

behind schedule   (2)—later than planned

bend over backwards to   (3)—(+ V) try very hard to accomplish something

to blow something   (15)—make a big mistake; ruin

break even (on something)   (4)—sell for the amount of money invested

break into   (8)—begin a project or career successfully

bring (someone) around   (9)—succeed in persuading; cause to agree

bring up   (9) (S)—suggest

bring up to date   (2) (S)—modernize; give all current information

by all means   (7)—certainly; of course

C

call for   (5)—require, demand

call off   (2) (S)—cancel, cause not to happen (+ N; + Verb + ing)

call the shots   (5)—have the authority in a situation; give orders

carry out   (2) (S)—fulfill a process; complete

catch on (to something)   (6)—understand after some time; realize

catch red-handed   (15) (S)—be found during the act of doing something wrong (occasionally used in a friendly way about an act of kindness)

catch up (on something)   (2)—try to be on schedule after going too slowly

catch up (with or to someone)   (12)—overtake; come equal with (*with* and *to* are equally possible)

change (one's) mind (about something)   (7)—change one's decision or opinion

check (up) on something   (14)—investigate

come around   (9)—begin to agree

come between (2 people)   (11)—cause difficulty in others' relationship

come through (for someone)   (3)—satisfy someone's need, often with difficulty

come up in the world   (4)—gain wealth, success, importance

come up with (something)   (13)—create after long work; find something special after difficulty

count on   (10)—depend on

crack down on (someone)   (5)—become very strict with

cream of the crop   (12)—the very best

cut corners   (15)—do something incompletely or carelessly

cut off   (11) (S)—stop communication; end a relationship

D

dawn on (someone)   (6)—understand after some time; realize (uses inanimate subjects only)

day in and day out   (1)—always; continually difficult

do a favor (for someone)   (3) (S)—do a kindness for someone

do over   (10) (S)—repeat an action, often because it was not done well the first time

do without (4)—manage without something to save money or because there isn't enough money for it

double-cross (someone) (11)—betray; break a trust

draw the line at (7)—not accept (+ V + ing or + N indicating the thing that's unacceptable)

draw up (something) (13) (S)—plan in detail, usually on paper

dream up (13) (S)—create in a very imaginative way

E

every now and then (1)—sometimes; not often

every so often (1)—sometimes; not often

F

face to face (12)—in the presence of; in person

fair and square (12)—with justice; not cheating

fall behind (on something) (2) (Int.)—to be slower than the schedule

fall through (2) (Int.)—fail to happen or be completed against one's will (only takes inanimate subjects)

figure out (something or someone) (6) (S)—understand after examination or thought; solve

fill in (6) (S)—give information; explain

fix up (something) (13) (S)—decorate; make more attractive or useful

fool around (15)—have fun, joke, play games; waste time; (also used: *mess around*)

for good (1)—forever (used especially with verbs meaning "finishing")

for the time being (1)—currently; for a short time; now

from now on (1)—from this moment, beginning now and continuing forever

G

gather from (something) (6)—understand based on information or evidence

to get (something) (6)—to understand

get (someone) in trouble (15)—put another person in a difficult position

get a/the jump on (someone or something) (12)—get an immediate advantage; start ahead of time (*a* and *the* are equally possible)

get across (9) (S)—explain successfully

get after (someone) (9)—try very hard to persuade someone (often used when the persuasion is considered impolite or too strong)

get ahead (8) (Int.)—become more successful; get a job promotion

get along (with someone) (11)—have a good relationship; be friendly

get away with something (15)—not be punished for wrongdoing

get back at someone (12)—get revenge

get carried away (with something) (14)—lose control because of excitement

get cold feet (about something) (8)—become so afraid that one can't do something

get even (with someone) (12)—get revenge

get in touch (with someone) (11)—communicate with; contact

get in trouble (15)—be punished for wrongdoing, put oneself in a difficult situation

get on someone's nerves (15)—annoy or bother someone

get one's (own) way (10)—get one's wish; win

get out from under (4)—recover from financial problems; pay all of one's bills

get out of hand (14)—become uncontrolled

get out of line (5)—disobey, cause trouble, misbehave

get rid of (7)—remove; send or throw away

get the better of (someone) (12)—defeat, get an advantage over

get through to someone (11)—communicate successfully

get to (8)—have a welcome opportunity (+ to + V)

get to the bottom of something (6)—understand the cause of a problem after investigation

get to the point (9)—speak directly

give (someone) a hand (3)—help

give a break (3) (S)—give a chance

give and take (3)—sharing; cooperation

give in (to something or someone) (9)—stop trying to persuade; agree to do as the opposition wishes (+ V + ing or + N)

give the cold shoulder (to someone) (11) (S)—be unfriendly; refuse to speak to

give up (on something) (10)—stop trying (+ V + ing)

go by the book (5)—do something according to the rules; not be creative or flexible

go for (something) (10)—try hard to achieve a much-wanted goal

go head to head with (someone over something) (12)—compete with directly, strongly

go off the deep end (14)—lose control over one's actions or emotions; do too much of something

go through (proper) channels (5)—follow the bureaucratic, formal procedures

go to any length (10)—do anything necessary to achieve something (+ to + V) (also, *go to great lengths*)

go without saying (that) (9)—it's obvious (+ noun clause) (subject is usually a noun clause or "it")

goof off (15) (Int.)—waste time (compare with *fool around*)

H

hand in hand (3)—together

have (something) going for (one) (8)—have an advantage or benefit

have a screw loose (15)—be strange, foolish, or crazy

have a voice in (7)—have a role in decision-making

have one's heart set on something (10)—want very, very much

have the last word (9)—make the final statement or decision in an argument

have two strikes against one (12)—have a difficulty that makes success unlikely (notice it does not have to be two difficulties; this comes from baseball terminology—three strikes and you're out)

have what it takes   (8)—be qualified, capable (+ to + V)

help out   (3) (S)—give assistance

hit on (something) (13)—find suddenly (used in discussing solutions to problems)

I

in one's way   (12)—able to stop one; a hindrance or problem (also, *in the way*)

in the long run   (1)—in the end; far into the future; eventually

in the red   (4)—in debt (opposite, *in the black*, not in debt)

in time   (1)—a) eventually, after some time; b) soon enough (+ to + V) (often used with *just* for emphasis)

J

jump at (something)   (8)—make immediate use of an opportunity

just around the corner   (1)—soon; an event very near in time

K

keep (on)   (10)—continue (+ V + ing)

keep a lid on something   (14)—control; stop from increasing

keep an eye on something or someone   (14)—watch carefully; pay careful attention to

keep in touch (with someone) (11)—maintain contact or communication

keep one's word   (3)—fulfill a promise

keep someone from   (12)—prevent (+ V + ing)

keep someone or something in line   (14)—maintain control over something or someone

keep tabs on something or someone   (14)—maintain knowledge of; maintain a record of

keep track of   (2)—maintain a written or mental record of; remember

keep up (with someone)   (12)—go at the same speed

kick around (something)   (13) (S)—discuss ideas as part of the creation or problem–solving process

knock it off   (15)—command to stop doing something objectionable (not polite; usually said in anger)

know the ropes   (6)—understand a procedure or system

L

land on one's feet   (4)—get out of trouble, often with an advantage

lay off   (4) (S)—temporarily dismiss someone from a job

let down (someone)   (15) (S)—to disappoint someone

live it up   (4)—spend money freely

look forward to   (2)—happily expect (+ Verb + ing or Noun)

look over   (7) (S)—examine carefully; study

lose one's head   (15)—lose self-control; become wild (compare with *get carried away* and *go off the deep end*, Ch. 14.)

lose one's touch   (13)—lose a creative ability

lose touch (with someone)   (11)—lose contact or communication, not on purpose

lose track of something or someone (14)—lose knowledge about; not have a record of

M

make a breakthrough (on something) (13)—find a solution after great difficulty

make a decision (about) (7)—decide; choose

make a fool of someone (15)—cause someone to look foolish

make a living by (4)—earn enough money to pay one's living expenses

make do with (something) (13)—manage with less than is usually necessary

make ends meet (4)—have enough money for expenses

make friends with someone (11)—establish a friendship

make fun of something or someone (15)—joke about unkindly; mock

make good (as something) (8)—succeed

make good time (2)—finish faster than usual or than expected

make out (6) (S)—recognize; understand from careful thought

make sense (out) of (6)—find a way to understand

make sure (10)—be determined that something happens (+ "that" clause)

make the most of something (10)—use to the greatest advantage

make up (one's) mind (about something) (7)—decide

make up (something) (13) (S)—invent; make by hand

make up with (someone) (11)—reestablish a good relationship after being angry

make waves (15)—cause trouble; make a process more difficult

meet (one) halfway (3)—compromise; cooperate by not demanding 100% of what one wants

mess up (15) (S)—ruin, spoil (also used: *screw up*)

might as well (8)—a good idea; equal or preferable to the alternative (+ V)

miss out (on something) (8)—lose an opportunity

miss the boat (8)—lose an opportunity

move back (2) (S)—schedule for a later time

move up (2) (S)—schedule for an earlier time

N

no matter (10)—it makes no difference; regardless (usually followed by *wh-* word

O

off and on (1)—sometimes; not often (used especially for actions that stop and start again)

on purpose (10)—intentionally; with planning

on second thought (7)—change a decision after thinking about it again

on the spur of the moment (2)—without planning or careful thought; impulsively

on time (1)—at the correct time

once and for all (10)—without doubt; definitely (argumentative, often indicates anger in conversation)

once in a while (1)—sometimes; not often

one way or another/the other (10)—in any way necessary for success

out of one's way (12)—unable to stop one; out of competition (also, *out of the way*)

out of the question (7)—absolutely impossible

P

pick up on something (6)—understand intuitively, from indirect information; understand or discover without trying

play (something) by ear (8)—deal with a situation as it happens, without planning

pull strings (5)—achieve a goal through unusual help from an important person

pull together (3) (Int.)—cooperate (requires plural subjects)

put an end to something (5)—cause something to stop

put down someone (11) (S)—show a lack of admiration or respect for someone; insult

put off (2) (S)—postpone: schedule for a later time (+ N; + Verb + ing)

put one's foot down (14)—refuse

put our or your heads together (13)—work together to create or find a solution

put up with someone or something (11)—accept a difficulty patiently; tolerate

R

read between the lines (6)—understand from what hasn't been said, indirectly

red tape (5)—complex bureaucratic procedures or paperwork (often used with the verb phrase "cut through," meaning to avoid or do quickly)

right away (1)—immediately

right-hand man or woman (3)—most helpful assistant

run (4)—cost

run out of (something) (4)—have no more in supply

S

scratch the surface (6)—understand only a little, superficially

see eye to eye (on something) (3)—agree

show off (something) (12) (S)—attract attention to oneself or one's belongings, usually impolitely

so far (1)—until now (uses present perfect or past perfect verb forms)

(not) stand a chance (8)—have a good opportunity or possibility (usually used in the negative or questions) (of + V + ing)

(not) stand for something (14)—(not) permit or allow; (not) tolerate

stand up for (9)—defend, support

strike out (8)—fail (past tense, struck) (comes from baseball: three strikes and the player is out)

T

take (someone or something) in hand (14)—establish control over someone or something to organize better

take care of (11)—fill someone's needs

take charge of something (14)—provide leadership; assume responsibility

take into account (7) (S)—consider when making a decision

take over something (14) (S)—assume complete control, often without permission

take shape (13)—develop gradually into the final form; evolve

take someone at his or her word (11)—believe what someone says without having any evidence; indicates doubt about truthfulness

take the bull by the horns (10)—attack a difficulty with determination

take turns (3)—alternate one after another (+ V + ing)

take up (something with someone) (5) (S)—discuss a problem with someone

talk back (to someone) (5)—answer disrespectfully

talk someone into something (9)—persuade someone to do something

talk someone out of something (9)—persuade someone not to do something

the ins and outs (6)—all the parts and their relationships (used with verbs of knowledge or understanding)

think twice (about) (7)—think very carefully about a difficult decision (+ V + ing) (*not think twice about* = have an easy decision)

think up (13)—create in an analytical way

throw the book at (5)—give the strongest punishment; talk to very strongly

toe the line (5)—obey; do one's duties; behave correctly

turn down (7) (S)—refuse; reject

W

waste one's breath (9)—explain or argue unsuccessfully

wear out (4)—no longer function

who's who (5)—who the important people are; everyone's identity

work out (13)—a) (S) to develop; b) (Int.) be successful

Answer Key

Chapter 1

EXERCISE 1:   2. F   4. T   6. T   8. F   10. F
EXERCISE 2:   2. c   4. a   6. b   8. c   10. b
EXERCISE 3:   2. N   4. N   6. Y   8. N   10. Y   12. Y
Answers to "Keep the Ball Rolling":   **A.** People in the U.S. generally expect guests to arrive no more than 5 or 10 minutes later than the scheduled time, especially for dinner. The exception is parties that will end late into the night.   **B.** It's considered rude in the U.S. to arrive early for any social engagement.   **C.** Last minute invitations are generally considered rude unless the host(ess) makes it clear that the whole engagement was conceived at the last minute.   **D.** People's job performance tends to be judged more on quantity and quality produced than on time spent at work in the U.S.   **E.** People in the U.S. generally plan uses for most of their time in advance. They <u>can</u> have plenty of time for personal conversation, but they usually like to plan time for that too.

Chapter 2

EXERCISE 1:   2. T   4. T   6. F   8. F   10. T   12. F   14. T
EXERCISE 2:   2. a   4. a   6. b   8. c   10. a
EXERCISE 3:   Hawaii <u>on the spur of the moment</u>, started to <u>keep track of</u>, Now we're <u>behind schedule</u>, 6 weeks to <u>catch up</u>, able to <u>carry out</u>, <u>(my uncle) to move up</u>, <u>am about to</u> go home

Chapter 3

EXERCISE 1:   2. T   4. F   6. T   8. F   10. F   12. T   14. F
EXERCISE 2:   2. a   4. a   6. c   8. c   10. b   12. b
EXERCISE 3:   compromise → <u>meet them halfway</u>, together → <u>hand in hand</u>, executive assistant → <u>right-hand man</u>, agree with each other → <u>see eye to eye</u>, work with each other → <u>pull together</u>

Chapter 4

EXERCISE 1:   2. b   4. b   6. a   8. b   10. a   12. b   14. a

EXERCISE 2: 2. a 4. b 6. b 8. b 10. a 12. c
EXERCISE 3: but I <u>am broke</u>, like to <u>live it up</u>, be able to <u>break even</u>, <u>came up in the world</u> only because of, clothes <u>wearing out</u>

Chapter 5

EXERCISE 1: 2. T 4. F 6. T 8. T 10. T 12. F 14. T
EXERCISE 2: 2. b 4. b 6. a 8. b 10. a 12. b 14. b
EXERCISE 3: *Possible answers:* 2. Throw the book at him anyway. 4. Take it up with your landlord. 6. Call for another election. 8. Unfortunately, the red tape is necessary. 10. Find out who's who at the *Gazette,* then try again.

Chapter 6

EXERCISE 1: 2. F 4. T 6. T 8. F 10. T 12. T
EXERCISE 2: scratched the surface, get to the bottom of, gathered from, add up, know the ropes, make out
EXERCISE 3: *Possible answers:* 2. Defense Claims Prosecution's Case Doesn't Add Up 4. Scientists Pick up on Signals of Galaxy's Birth 6. Secretary of State to Fill in President on China Trip 8. New Book Gets to the Bottom of Kids' Lies

Chapter 7

EXERCISE 1: 2. F 4. T 6. T 8. T 10. T 12. T
EXERCISE 2: 2. c 4. c 6. b 8. b 10. b 12. c
EXERCISE 3: examined → <u>looked over</u>, decided → <u>made up my mind</u>, remove → <u>get rid of</u>, have a role in → <u>have a voice in</u>, of course → <u>by all means</u>, think again about → <u>think twice about</u>

Chapter 8

EXERCISE 1: 2. T 4. F 6. F 8. T 10. T 12. F 14. F
EXERCISE 2: 2. have a lot going for 4. up for grabs 6. jumped at 8. struck out 10. might as well
EXERCISE 3: *Possible answers:* 2. Let's break into it! 4. No. I'll play it by ear. 6. They got cold feet! 8. Yep. We struck out! 10. Jump at it before it's too late!

Chapter 9

EXERCISE 1: 2. F 4. T 6. T 8. T 10. T 12. F 14. F
EXERCISE 2: when you <u>beat around the bush</u>; you're just <u>wasting your breath</u>; It goes without saying that the couch; Bob, I <u>gave in</u>; always has to <u>have the last word</u>; <u>come around</u> on his own; <u>back down</u> either
EXERCISE 3: *Possible answers:* 2. Benny's father wants Benny to get to the point. 4. Benny is trying to get his idea across. 6. Benny brings up his plan—to join the army. 8. Benny's mother tries to talk him out of the army. 10. Benny's mom has the last word.

Chapter 10

EXERCISE 1: 2. F 4. T 6. F 8. T 10. T 12. T 14. T
EXERCISE 2: 2. c 4. c 6. a 8. a 10. a
EXERCISE 3: let him <u>get his own way</u>, another person <u>on purpose</u>, <u>no matter what</u> he tells you, <u>given up on</u> enforcing, <u>count on</u> you for help, <u>go for</u> a business degree, know <u>once and for all</u>

Chapter 11

EXERCISE 1: 2. T   4. F   6. F   8. T   10. T   12. F   14. T   16. T
EXERCISE 2: that you <u>doubled crossed</u> her, how to <u>get through</u> to her, hard to put up with, promised to <u>keep in touch</u>, we're <u>in the same boat</u>, can't <u>get along with</u>, trying to <u>come between</u>, <u>make friends</u> without Tim's
EXERCISE 3: 2. In the Same Boat   4. Putting up with it   6. Making Up
8. Taking Care of Someone

Chapter 12

EXERCISE 1: 2. T   4. T   6. T   8. T   10. T   12. F   14. T   16. F
EXERCISE 2: wanted to <u>get back at</u>, <u>keep up with the Bulldogs</u>, Mad-Dog <u>face to face</u>, <u>play fair and square</u>, <u>get even with</u> him for cheating, <u>get the better of Jimmy</u>, prefer to talk <u>face to face</u>
EXERCISE 3: compete against → <u>go head to head with</u>, some disadvantages → <u>has two strikes against it</u>, in the contest → <u>in the running</u>, defeat → <u>get the better of</u>, hindered his success → <u>got in his way</u>

Chapter 13

EXERCISE 1: people to <u>put their heads together</u>, even <u>make a breakthrough</u>, like to <u>draw up</u>, have a <u>dry run</u>
EXERCISE 2: 2. b   4. a   6. a   8. c   10. c
EXERCISE 3: *Sentences are numbered as they appear in the exercise. X = <u>You figure it out</u>.*
4 × 9 × 1 × 5 × 8 × 11 ×
Answer to <u>"Keep the Ball Rolling"</u>: The solution is not letting the directions get in your way. For example, you weren't told there couldn't be 3-dimensional solutions, such as folding the paper and inserting the pencil through the dots or rolling the paper into a cone and doing the same. What other solutions can you come up with that seem to break the rules but don't really?

Chapter 14

EXERCISE 1: 2. F   4. T   6. F   8. F   10. T   12. T   14. F
EXERCISE 2: 2. a   4. c   6. c   8. c   10. a
EXERCISE 3: 2. g   4. l   6. i   8. e   10. o   12. h   14. j

Chapter 15

EXERCISE 1: 2. T   4. F   6. T   8. T   10. F   12. F   14. F   16. T
EXERCISE 2: fool around → <u>waste time</u>, get away with it → <u>don't get punished</u>, gets on my nerves → <u>bothers me</u>, have a screw loose → <u>be foolish</u>, goof off → <u>waste time</u>
EXERCISE 3: 2. Getting on her Nerves   4. Fooling Around   6. Getting Caught Red-handed   8. Losing His Head